PUBLIC WAR, PRIVATE CONSCIENCE

Also available from Continuum:

Ethics: Key Concepts in Philosophy, Dwight Furrow
Humanity, Terrorism, Terrorist War, Ted Hondcrich
Israel, Palestine and Terror, edited by Stephen Law
Terrorism, Nicholas Fotion, Boris Kashnikov and Joanne K. Lekea
War and Ethics, Nicholas Fotion
The Ethics of Torture, J. Jeremy Wisnewski and R.D. Emerick

PUBLIC WAR, PRIVATE CONSCIENCE

THE ETHICS OF POLITICAL VIOLENCE

ANDREW FIALA

continuum

Continuum International Publishing Group

The Tower Building	80 Maiden Lane
11 York Road	Suite 704
London SE1 7NX	New York, NY 10038

www.continuumbooks.com

British Library Cataloguing-in-Publication Data
A catalogue record for this book is available from the British Library.

ISBN: HB: 978-1-4411-8258-6
PB: 978-1-4411-8281-4

Library of Congress Cataloging-in-Publication Data
Fiala, Andrew G. (Andrew Gordon), 1966-
Public war, private conscience : the ethics of
political violence / Andrew Fiala.
p. cm.
Includes bibliographical references.
ISBN-13: 978-1-4411-8258-6 (hbk.)
ISBN-10: 1-4411-8258-6 (hbk.)
ISBN-13: 978-1-4411-8281-4 (pbk.)
ISBN-10: 1-4411-8281-0 (pbk.)
1. War–Moral and ethical aspects. 2. Political violence–Moral and ethical aspects. 3. Terrorism. 4. Conscientious objection. 5. Just war doctrine. 6. Pacifism. 7. War (Philosophy) 8. Utilitarianism. 9. Duty. I. Title.
U22.F49 2010
172'.42–dc22
2009041193

Typeset by Newgen Imaging Systems Pvt Ltd, Chennai, India
Printed and bound in Great Britain by the MPG Books Group

CONTENTS

PREFACE

This is our cry. This is our prayer. Peace in the world.
Children's Peace Memorial, Hiroshima

Some years after the atomic bomb was dropped on Hiroshima, a girl named Sadako Sasaki was diagnosed with leukemia that was attributed to radiation from the bomb. According to Japanese legend, if one folded 1,000 paper cranes, a wish might be granted. So Sadako began to fold origami cranes. Unfortunately, legends do not cure cancer and Sadako died in 1955 at the age of 12. After her death, Sadako's friends continued to fold paper cranes. In Hiroshima today, paper cranes are ubiquitous symbols of the hope for peace.

War is especially horrifying when it hurts children. But children are easy targets. They get caught in the crossfire. They step on land mines and are victims of bombing attacks. They are used as human shields, coerced into suicide missions, and conscripted into military service. And they suffer most from the instability produced by war. A recent study indicates that in Afghanistan, after 25 years of conflict, children experience high levels of post-traumatic stress disorder (Catani, 2009). And according to UNICEF's *Child Alert on Afghanistan* (2007), Afghanistan has one of the highest infant and childhood mortality rates in the world. Similar suffering can be seen among children in war zones across the globe.

This brings us back to Sadako and the especially poignant suffering of children during war. Childhood is a special, sacred zone of privacy. That is why a child's suffering is such a tragic loss. When the bomb exploded over Hiroshima, Sadako was an infant—entirely innocent of any of the crimes committed by the Japanese Empire. And yet she was swept away by the international strife that culminated in the mushroom cloud.

In 2007, I traveled to Hiroshima to participate in a conference on international dialogue, war, and peace. At that time, reaction against the United States and the invasion of Iraq was quite strong. Some of the participants in the conference argued that what happened in Hiroshima in 1945 was linked to what happened in Iraq in 2003—with American Imperial aspirations resulting in unjust wars and atrocities. American power has indeed spread via military force: from the Mexican and Indian wars to the annexation of Hawaii and the Philippines, from the World Wars to Korea, Vietnam, and on to Afghanistan and Iraq. But the usual criticism of American Imperialism misses the more disturbing fact that the atrocity of Hiroshima and the debacle of Iraq were grounded in a deep commitment to noble principles. These were not cases of evil people doing evil things for the sake of evil. Rather, the problem is that the history of American Imperialism shows us that good people do horrible things for the sake of the good.

It is easier to believe that evil acts are done by evil people. Some evils are obvious. It is simply wrong to persuade a 6 year old to wear a suicide vest, telling him that it will spray out flowers if he presses a button—as apparently has happened in Afghanistan (UNICEF, 2007). But the depressing conclusion is that evil is often committed in the name of the good. It is easier to make sense of a straightforward account of evil in which wrongdoers are psychopathic and sadistic. It is much harder to make sense of a world in which good people do horrible things in the name of good causes. And yet, in Hiroshima—as in Baghdad and Kabul—this is what we discover. The distressing problem is that the public logic of war is fundamentally at odds with the moral logic of private life.

This problem was noted recently by President Barack Obama, as he accepted the Nobel Peace Prize in 2009. Obama acknowledged that the challenge is to reconcile "two seemingly irreconcilable truths": "that war is sometimes necessary, and war at some level is an expression of human folly." From the standpoint of the public good, war can appear as a necessary response to evil. But from the standpoint of the individual, war appears as folly, horror, and madness. I fear that Obama is correct: that there is no easy way to reconcile these rival points of view.

The more I work on this topic, the more difficult it becomes. Indeed, the longer I study the human condition, the more bewildered I am. There are no easy answers to our most important questions.

Life is complicated, tragic, and uncertain. Nothing shows us this better than war. War contains noble sacrifices and horrible misdeeds, it brings out the best and the worst in human nature. In war, great evils occasionally produce great goods. And in war, good will can go horribly awry. My interest in war is "philosophical" in the sense that reflection on war is also reflection on life, its conflicting interests, competing values, and tragic dilemmas.

The paradigm conflict that I will examine throughout this book is the conflict between public and private, between the individual and the state. War is carried out by individuals but organized by states. In war, the majesty of the state exerts itself against the interests of individuals. In peacetime, state power remains latent—more implicit than explicit, more a whisper than a shout. We pay our taxes, obey the speed limit, and benefit from collective action in schools and in parks. In peacetime, it is easy to ignore the quiet presence of the state and imagine a world of individuals coexisting in communal harmony.

But war rips open the façade of community, reminding us that violent conflict is always possible. In war, the state demands much more than taxes and obedience—it now requires sacrifices of life and liberty. In war, the state can use individuals as soldiers, taking young men and women from their jobs, their homes, and their families and ending their lives on foreign streets. And in war, innocent bystanders come to be seen as collateral damage: children are killed, families are destroyed, and widows are created.

The sacrifices of war appear insane from the peaceful standpoint of private life. Why should a child ever be killed or orphaned? In the name of what higher value can this ever be justified? And so, pacifism remains a compelling ethical and philosophical ideal. But if pacifists refuse to compromise with the dehumanizing violence of state power, they should—to be consistent—also refuse the benefits of state power. A consistent pacifism must also be a sort of anarchism that is content with the sorts of goods that can be attained from a very primitive and minimal form of social organization.

But very few of us would be content with a life of Franciscan poverty or Amish simplicity. We enjoy the benefits of the modern state—universities and science projects, transportation infrastructure, and international commerce. But these goods are produced by a centralized state, which has the power to declare war in defense of public good, the power to use individuals for the good of the whole.

Hiroshima is one of the best places to witness the conflict of war and peace, public and private. On August 6, 1945, the American B-29 bomber, Enola Gay, dropped an atomic bomb named "Little Boy," which exploded over Hiroshima, instantly killing 70,000 people. Another 100,000 Japanese—including Sadako—died within the next several years from burns, cancers, and radiation sickness. Our memory of this public atrocity is haunted by the subtle niceties of private life—from the shadows of human beings that were left when bodies were incinerated to the pocket watch stopped forever at 8:15 a.m., the time of the detonation. Even the cute name of the bomb and the name of the B-29 remind us of the personal and private: the plane was named after Enola Gay Tibbets, the mother of the pilot Paul Tibbets. The human mind, it seems, cannot grasp an atrocity of this magnitude directly. Instead, we focus on the personal details and the private nature of suffering: from Enola Gay and "Little Boy" to the stopped watch and Sadako's cranes.

In the aftermath of the Second World War, the international system as we know it developed. The United States rebuilt Japan after its own image. And in the postwar period, the horror of nuclear weapons and the memory of Hiroshima worked to foster the unstable peace of the Cold War. Although small-scale hot wars erupted in Asia and elsewhere, the nuclear powers thankfully refrained from pursuing the logic of war all the way toward mutually assured destruction. That gives us reason to hope. But it is a sad fact of human nature that it took the absolute horror of total war to provide the beginning of peace. The most disturbing fact about human beings is that the flower of peace could only begin to bloom in the shadow of the mushroom cloud.

When I visited Hiroshima, I was deeply disturbed by the peaceful and beautiful park that has flourished in the footprint of the bomb. The epicenter of the atomic bomb attacks is now a charming place in which tourists from around the world mingle and reflect. One corner of this park contains a repository for the thousands of carefully folded and multicolored paper cranes, which children from across Japan and the world send to Hiroshima in memory of the children who died and in hope of peace. These paper cranes are beautiful symbols of the hopeful innocence of childhood. If you go to Hiroshima, you will undoubtedly be given or learn to fold one of these origami cranes. But no amount of folded paper can make up for thousands of children burned alive or dying of cancer.

It is disquieting that history appeared to require the horrors of the bomb and the rest of the horrors of the World War to arrive at the serenity of the children's paper crane memorial. How sad that humanity could do no better than this: that generations of child victims of war had to be burned, orphaned, and dismembered on the slaughter-bench of war so that children today might join together in peace. Why is it that human beings could not imagine a better way? And why can't we do better today?

The serene tranquility of the Hiroshima Peace Park and the Hiroshima Peace Memorial rests upon the exact spot where a singular event of mass murder occurred. When I was in Hiroshima in 2007, children were playing musical instruments in a concert on the shores of the Ota River, in the very shadow of the Atomic Bomb Dome—the skeletal wreckage that has been preserved as a monument to the destruction of the bomb. Street vendors worked in the park. Lovers walked hand in hand. Laughter and song wafted across a landscape that was once the site of mass slaughter.

The grotesque sublimity of the world is captured in the fact that a beautiful park can grow out of a landscape desolated by the worst weapon of mass destruction ever used. How bizarre that citizens of countries who once fought to the death are now allies and friends. How unnerving that warriors, heroes, and children die in agony and despair, only to leave behind the somewhat banal and mundane landscape of peace.

This book is motivated by this sense of the disturbing weirdness of a world in which mushroom clouds turn into paper cranes. In the world as I see it, there can be no final resolution or explanation of the hideous evil of war. It is impossible to explain or justify a soldier's death to his child, mother, or wife. And it is even more impossible to explain or justify a child's death either at the hands of a deluded terrorist or beneath the wings of just warriors who fight in defense of noble goods. There are moral distinctions to be made here: terrorism is wrong and violence may be permitted in self-defense. But a child remains absolutely dead, whether killed by a terror bomber or as collateral damage in a legitimate war of self-defense.

The more I've thought about the just war theory and its attempts at justification and explanation, the more suspicious I am that this theory only really works if it is combined with some sort of theodicy. Theodicies attempt to explain how a good and all-powerful God can permit evil. In the book of Job, God provides the clearest answer: there is no explanation for evil. Bad things happen to good people: children are killed as collateral damage, terrorists destroy magnificent skyscrapers, and heroic soldiers are killed by friendly fire. Justifications can be given for these tragedies. But in the end, the fact of loss and evil remain. According to Job, the human task is simply to admit the fact of evil and resign oneself to the incomprehensible will of God.

There is wisdom in Job. But the conclusion is unsatisfying. We cannot simply resign ourselves to the death of children. There is a deep and abiding urge to seek to explain and justify in the face of atrocity. This urge leads us toward concepts such as good and evil, justice and injustice. Without these concepts, we are absolutely bereft. Job's conclusion is a kind of bereavement: he repents in dust and ashes and completely gives himself up to God. But this approach cannot get us very far in a world that requires judgment and action. The just war theory is our best attempt at applying moral judgment to war.

But we must be careful as we employ moral language and act upon our moral judgments. Moral terms are often disconnected from the reality of suffering and loss. And moral language can be abused by those in power. Unreflective judgment, moralistic obtuseness, and careless action are just as bad as deliberate evil. The philosophical tradition teaches us, in opposition to the faith of Job, that we need to develop moral wisdom in order to make good judgments. But the philosophical tradition also reminds us that we often do not completely understand the meaning of the moral terms we employ. This is why self-criticism is continually required.

Concepts such as good and evil are useful and easy to apply in some circumstances. Evil is obvious in the intentional and deliberate torture and genocidal slaughter of the death camps in Nazi Germany, the killing fields of Cambodia, the gulags of the Soviet Union, the streets of Rwanda, the countryside of Darfur. It is also obvious at "ground zero" in Hiroshima and in lower Manhattan. Genocide and indiscriminate mass slaughter are wrong, unjust, evil. There are no excuses for genocide, no way to rationalize terrorism.

But the evil of Hiroshima is different and more difficult to deal with than the evil of Auschwitz or Rwanda. At Hiroshima, we do not witness the deliberate evil of genocidal slaughter that was generated by a deliberately cruel and merciless *Weltanschauung*. Rather, at Hiroshima, we witness the even more disturbing malady of good intentions gone horribly awry. One cannot use the term "evil" to describe the events at Hiroshima in the same way that the term can be employed in describing Auschwitz or Rwanda. But what occurred at Hiroshima was still a deliberate atrocity, in which the aim was to kill as many persons as possible. The use of incendiary bombs across Japan as well as a second atomic bomb dropped on Nagasaki were part of a deliberate strategy of destruction that was essential to American victory in what is commonly described as "the good war." And here is the problem: at Hiroshima we see the gruesome reality that a supposedly just war can culminate in mass murder.

The Japanese were aggressive. They were motivated by a state centered, racial ideology. They raped captive women and slaughtered innocents. Their doctors engaged in horrifying medical experiments on prisoners. And they generally violated the conventions of war. The war against Japan was a justifiable response to Japanese aggression and injustice. The Japanese deserved to be defeated. And the conversion of Japan to liberal democracy was a progressive development.

But none of this can justify the death of Japanese children under the black sun of the mushroom cloud or the subsequent distress of the survivors who suffered from burns and cancers, folding paper cranes as their bodies were slowly destroyed by radiation poisoning.

The problem I am describing here is not unique to Japan or Hiroshima or even to war, even though it is made most palpable in Hiroshima. The problem is that individuals are literally used up in pursuit of public goods. Life is lived in the first-person from the standpoint of the individual. But individuals are also members of larger social wholes. And these social wholes proceed by a logic of their own in which individuals are merely members or cells of the social body. When the health of the larger organism requires it, these cells are sloughed off and the members are sacrificed for the good of the whole. War is only the most obvious and horrifying example of this unhandsome fact.

This book attempts to reflect on this sort of conflict and disturbance. It brings together a variety of threads, including the following.

First, it aims to recount a historical development in the Western tradition: from the ancient world in which individuals were viewed primarily as members of the whole to the contemporary liberal view which holds that individuals have inalienable rights over against the needs of the collective. The liberal ideal is only a late development in human history. But it is an important development that may help us move beyond war. I attempt to explain the connection between liberal values and progress toward peace.

Second, the book aims to provide insight into a very basic conflict in ethical theory. On the one hand, the deontological approach to ethics is based on a conception of the absolute duties of private life, which demand respect for the inherent value of individuals. On the other hand, the utilitarian approach is interested in working to maximize the greatest happiness for the greatest number of people. I show how these rival approaches provide divergent ways of thinking about the ethics of war. And I use war as a lens to see how these divergent views of ethics remain in conflict.

Third, the book attempts to provide some unique insights into a variety of prominent philosophers in our tradition. War was a primary concern for many philosophers in the Western tradition. This fact is often overlooked in standard accounts of the history of philosophy. I try to remedy this by looking deeper into the way that war has been a central issue for philosophers from Heraclitus to the present.

Finally, the book attempts to reflect upon current affairs and contemporary conflicts, with a special focus on the war on terrorism, the use of torture, and the question of conscientious objection in a professional/volunteer army. It also attempts to connect philosophical theory to historical reality—in discussions of the Peloponnesian War, the American Revolution, the Civil War, American Imperialism, the World Wars, Korea, and Vietnam. These events impacted philosophical thinking in a variety of ways, which I try to take into account.

This book is one more paper crane, folded in the shadow of the cloud of war. It is a small attempt to make sense of the world and provide hope. But my conclusion is that there are no easy answers and no satisfying theodicies. Life is hard. Moral judgment is difficult. And evil happens despite our best intentions. This is a bleak conclusion. But it is honest. The hope is that in being honest about the human predicament, we may continue to make progress— slow excruciating progress—toward unfolding a better world.

ACKNOWLEDGMENTS

This book was written over the course of several years. Many of its ideas were honed at conferences. I would like to thank colleagues for their feedback at meetings of the International Society for Universal Dialogue, the American Academy of Religion, the International Society for Military Ethics, and especially the Society for Philosophy in the Contemporary World.

A few of the chapters represent significant revisions of articles that I've previously published. Chapter Six is a significant revision of "The Democratic Peace Myth: From Hiroshima to Baghdad" in Edward Demenchonok, ed., *Between Global Violence and Ethics of Peace: Philosophical Perspectives* (Malden, MA: Wiley-Blackwell Publishing, 2009). Thanks to Edward Demenchonok for his feedback on that article. Chapter Seven is a significant revision of "The Vanity of Temporal Things: Hegel and the Ethics of War" in *Studies in the History of Ethics* (February 2006). And Chapter Ten is a significant revision of "Waterboarding, Torture, and Violence: Normative Definitions and the Burden of Proof" in *Review Journal of Political Philosophy*, special issue: "Torture, Terrorism, and the Use of Violence" 6:1 (Fall 2008). Thanks to Jeremy Wisnewski for his editorial assistance on that article.

Many others helped me with feedback and suggestions on bits and pieces of this book. Thanks especially to Derek Jeffreys, David Chan, Dane Scott, Rob Metcalf, Courtney Campbell, Joseph Orosco, and Lani Roberts—for stimulating conversations, inspirational ideas, and for providing opportunities to share my work.

Finally, as always, thanks to Julaine, Gordon, Peggy, Don, Valerie, Tahoe, and Bodhi.

CHAPTER ONE

THE SUBLIME GRIND OF ARES

You—I hate you most of all the Olympian gods. Always dear to your heart, strife, yes, and battles, the bloody grind of war.
Homer, Iliad *(Book 5, 1027–1032)*

War uses up and grinds down individuals. War is a public event and a political process with overwhelming sublime power. It is an organized and sustained activity that coordinates masses of human beings in a way that is necessarily disrespectful of individuality. While societies mobilize and organize individuals in a variety of other endeavors—for education, science, public health, and economics—war is unique insofar as it blatantly uses individuals and uses them up in the process. War is highly organized and hierarchical: it is *cosmos* in the Greek sense of the term—it is ordered and structured. But war is also *chaos* or disorder incarnate: a flurry of indiscriminate destruction. In war, the ordered hierarchy of military and political power is aimed purely and simply at efficiency in destruction: a dance of cosmos and chaos. In this dance, individuals are trampled under and ground down but also lifted up and transcended in service to the larger whole.

War is *sublime*, in the sense of this term explained by Immanuel Kant, the great philosopher of the Enlightenment. War exhilarates and uplifts despite its very atrocity and terror. In war, individuals confront their fragility and finitude and are oddly enough lifted beyond themselves, despite the fact that war grinds them down to nothing. Here is how Kant connects war to the idea of the sublime in the *Critique of Judgment*:

> War itself, if it is carried on with order and with sacred respect for the rights of citizens, has something sublime in it, and makes the disposition of the people who carry it on thus, only the more sublime, the more numerous are the dangers to which they are exposed, and in respect of which they behave with courage. (Kant, 1970, § 28, 102)

Kant's understanding of the sublime is directly related to his idea of morality. Morality lifts us beyond ourselves toward unconditioned duty: beyond happiness and inclination toward respect for the moral law. Kant says in the *Groundwork of the Metaphysics of Morals* that the "sublimity and inner dignity" of the moral law is made clearest when the moral law requires obedience that is opposed to subjectivity and self-interest (Kant, 1998a, 35). One obvious example of this sort of obedience and duty is found in military service, in which the soldier sacrifices himself in duty for the greater good—despite his inclinations, fears, and self-interest. War, like morality itself, is thus uncanny and sublime.

Individuality is destroyed in war; but individuality is also fulfilled through service and sacrifice to the greater good. War is terrifying and chaotic; but war can foster courage, while producing a kind of order. War produces horror, while allowing for glory. War produces a public good but is a threat to private conscience. These sorts of dichotomies are the focus of the present inquiry.

Kant is usually thought of as a pacifist. Along with other philosophers of the Enlightenment—Rousseau and Bentham, for example—Kant advocated a plan for perpetual peace that would bring about the end of war. So it is significant that Kant recognizes the sublime power of war. Despite his hope for perpetual peace, Kant also sees something degenerate and effeminate in peace. "A long peace generally brings about a predominant commercial spirit, and along with it, low selfishness, cowardice, and effeminacy, and debases the disposition of the people" (Kant, 1970, 102). Kant also recognizes that war can be a progressive mechanism for human history (Kant, 1970, § 83). The contradiction contained in Kant's view cannot be downplayed: war is horrible and ugly but it also contains a sublime power that can be used for good purposes; peace

2

is a good we all hope for but peace can be connected with selfishness, cowardice, and effeminacy.

The gendered language is telling. War and public service are viewed as masculine, while peace and privacy are viewed as feminine. This gendered language reflects a major dichotomy in our thinking about war, politics, and the good. Indeed, as we shall see, the world's philosophical and religious traditions express deep ambivalence about war.

PRIVATE INDIVIDUALITY AND THE GENERAL GOOD

War sacrifices some individuals for the common good. War requires individuality to be subordinated to the centralized authority who deploys groups of individual soldiers in order to destroy other similar groups of individuals. The persons who make up the war machine are viewed as mere parts of the whole, to be used (and used up, if necessary) for the good of the whole.

This structure is disclosed in the very language of the military hierarchy, where "privates" are deployed by "generals." In the feudal period, "private soldiers" were hired or conscripted by feudal lords for military service. They remained merely "private" insofar as they were not of noble birth: they did not have the power to take account of the public good. In this sense, private men are deprived of a significant good: they are unable to participate in public discourse or take account of the public good. We see this idea in Shakespeare's *Henry V*, where the king laments his public role and pines for the ease of private life:

> What infinite heart's ease must kings neglect
> That private men enjoy?
> And what have kings that privates have not too,
> Save ceremony, save general ceremony? (Act IV, Scene i)

Shakespeare indicates that even the king himself must sacrifice his private ease for public service. Private enjoyment gives way to the obligations of public service and war produces dis-ease.

Despite King Henry's longing for the ease of private life, the fact was that in the medieval period, private men could be conscripted and employed by the state. The idea that the state can use private men for public purposes gradually changed through the Enlightenment and the democratic revolutions of the eighteenth

3

and nineteenth centuries. This shift was produced by a change in our understanding of the relative import of public and private, to the point where private life was defended as a bastion of liberty against the intrusion of public concern. Although conscription continued throughout the mass wars of the twentieth century, it was eventually abolished in the United States, as a violation of liberty. President Nixon—who was himself a Shakespearean figure—explained the problem of conscription as follows in his message to Congress on draft reform (April 23, 1970):

> By upholding the cause of freedom without conscription we will have demonstrated in one more area the superiority of a society based upon belief in the dignity of man over a society based on the supremacy of the State.

It took many long centuries to arrive at the conclusion that the dignity of man created a limit on state power that even included limits on drafting private individuals into state service. Despite the abolition of the draft, the tension between private interest and public service remains. There are values to be obtained in public service; and the very idea of privacy is etymologically related to the idea of deprivation. In his reflection on the emergence of the modern idea of public and private, Jürgen Habermas explains how the "common" man and "private" soldier were seen as lacking something. The private soldier was "the ordinary man without rank and without the particularity of a special power to command interpreted as 'public'" (Habermas, 1991, 6). The feudal lord was the public man who had the privilege—and heartache and responsibility—of public service. This public or general standpoint is the purview of the general in today's military. Generals deal with masses of men, while the private's concern is himself alone.

Hierarchy and centralization are essential in war. War literally demands that the private submit to the general, that individuals submit to the concerns of the greater good. War uses both kings and privates for the greater good. The dehumanizing aspect of military service is the way that it uses individuals in this way. But at the same time, military service can also be progressive and socially constructive insofar as it establishes a sort of equality in service, which Shakespeare indicated in the famous "band of brothers" speech from *Henry V.* King Henry proclaims equality in service as the shed blood of each soldier lifts each above his station, making them all "gentle" (i.e., gentlemen): "For he to-day that sheds his blood with me shall be my brother; be he ne'er so vile, this day shall gentle his condition" (Act IV, Scene iii).

Soldiers share as brothers in the common struggle, despite differences in rank or social class. In this sense, war and military service can have a democratizing outcome, despite the fact of hierarchy in the military. Thus, one danger of the abolition of the draft has been the way in which the volunteer military has tended to become less representative of society as a whole. It is an odd development in world history that the army of the global superpower is made up of volunteers who either are often much more conservative than the mainstream population or who are not themselves citizens. Meanwhile the majority of citizens enjoy the ease of private life, without engaging in any of the burdens of public service.

INDIVIDUALITY AND HEROISM

War reminds us of the fact that individuality is ephemeral and insignificant. Some individuals are apparently rescued from the grind of war when they are celebrated as heroes. Individuals do have an opportunity to develop virtue in the face of battle: cleverness, integrity, loyalty, and courage are forged and tested in the crucible of war. But warriors rarely choose the cause for which they fight; nor do they choose the battles into which they are thrown or the tactics employed. These choices are made by military and political authorities, not by individual soldiers.

The hero is the exception to the impersonal and collective logic of war. Heroes are celebrated as individuals of character, intelligence, and talent. But in war, heroism is often a matter of contingent circumstance. It is true that soldiers can exhibit exceptional courage, stamina, and fortitude. But in contemporary warfare, individual fighters have very little to say about where, when, and how they fight. War is a mass movement of men; heroism is primarily a matter of moral luck. In battle, survival and success are dependent upon a variety of conditions over which the individual soldier has very little control. The solider cannot control material conditions, such as weather and equipment. Nor can he control social conditions, such as tactical and strategic planning or morale. Individual heroism only occurs when the social force of war and the contingencies of fate allow it. Some heroes are killed by friendly fire, as Pat Tillman was. Others, such as Audie Murphy, get lucky and manage to succeed despite the odds against them. Even the most disciplined, courageous, and well-trained soldier is still buffeted by the winds of fortune and the tidal forces of history.

Audie Murphy himself—the most decorated hero of the Second World War— recognized that in war the individual is a mere cog in the machine. In his account of the war, Murphy describes leading his men into battle with the following description.

> Right now I am concerned with the individual only as a fighting unit. If his feet freeze, I will turn him over to the medics. If his nerves crack, I will send him to the rear. If he is hit, I will see that his wound is treated. Otherwise, I look upon him as a unit whom I must get to the front and in battle position on schedule. (Murphy, 2002, 253)

War is a social force and historical event that uses individuals as units to be moved into position. And it must be this way. In wartime, the state simply cannot view individuals as persons with inherent dignity and absolute worth. The officers who lead the fighting must, like Murphy, view the privates as fungible assets to be deployed as necessary. War is about nations, armies, crowds, mobs, and random bunches of human beings. The individuals who make up these groups are exchangeable, replaceable, substitutable units. They are so many parts that can be moved, assembled, and disassembled. The focus of politics is the nation, the state, and the common good. The focus of military science is the squad, the company, the battalion, the brigade, and the army. The individual soldier or citizen is only relevant as a unit within these larger groups. From the point of view of war as a mass movement, the concerns and interests of individual soldiers are irrelevant. War cares little for the character, virtue, motives, or intentions of the individual soldiers. Some fight out of hatred, some out of a sense of justice, some for the money, and some because they have nothing better to do. The state and the military are not concerned with these morally relevant differences, so long as the movement of the whole remains coherent.

In the ethics of war, the only moral distinction among individuals that matters is the very general and slippery one between combatant and noncombatant. But this distinction tells us little about the merit or value of the individuals who die or live. Some combatants are frightened and coerced. They may rather not fight; but so long as they wear the uniform and insignia of a combatant, they can legitimately be killed. At the same time, some noncombatants are bad guys who might deserve killing even though they do not bear arms or wear a uniform. The general rule of thumb is that soldiers may be killed—since they are the direct and immediate means by which war is waged; and noncombatants—captains of industry and the mothers and wives of soldiers—cannot be killed. This rule of thumb shows us the bluntness of moral distinctions in war. The fearful, conscripted youth is a legal target; but his fanatical uncle or patriotic mother is not. Moreover, even this rule of thumb can be scrapped in the midst of battle under the permissive rubric of collateral damage and by sophisticated application of the doctrine of double effect. Mothers, wives, and graying uncles can be killed in war, so long as their deaths are not directly intended or so long as there is a supreme emergency that gives us a reason to set our ethical rule of thumb aside.

War is not sensitive to the motives, intentions, and moral commitments of the individuals who are caught in its path. Wars proceed by a mechanistic utilitarian logic that is unable to consider the needs, desires, and stories of the individuals—combatants or noncombatants—who are ground down in the battle. Like the earthquake and the hurricane, war levels everything without regard for subtle moral distinctions. Some are spared, some are not; but life and death, disaster and salvation have little to do with merit or morality.

The private concerns of individual conscience are irrelevant to the public concerns of war. Thus, war exposes a tragic conflict between the general point of view of the common good and the particular point of view of the private soldier, between the public goods of political life and the private concerns of individual conscience.

IT DOES NOT KILL; NOR IS IT KILLED

The ancients believed that war was like a force of nature. Earthquakes and hurricanes and other forces of nature are sublime in the Kantian sense: they remind us of our fragility and finitude while also exhilarating us with their immense power. This may be why the ancients thought of war as a god. Just as Poseidon was the god of the earthquake, Ares or Polemos was the personification of war. In his translation of Homer's *Iliad*, Robert Fagles repeatedly speaks of "the grind of war," "the grind of Ares." Homer imagines war as a grinding stone that breaks down the hardened kernels of personality, combining individuals into a homogeneous mass. This motif continues in Aristophanes' play, *Peace*. In that comedy, War (Polemos) carries a huge mortar. He throws Greek cities into the mortar along with leeks, garlic, and other symbolic spices. His goal is to grind up or pound down the Greek cities and turn them into hash. In the comedy, Polemos can't find a proper pestle to do the pounding; so he goes off to create one. This provides the opportunity for Peace, the goddess, to be rescued. In reality, the mortar and pestle of the Peloponnesian War had already ground down upon the Greeks. The image of the grind of war is thus apropos. In its most extreme form, war literally turns human beings into hash: piles of corpses, blood, and body parts. Individuals are transformed from men who bear arms to heaps of arms and other body parts.

The Greeks were not the only ones to recognize the grind of war. In the Hindu epic, the *Bhagavad Gita*, the warrior Arjuna is troubled by the moral complexity of war and he pauses before commencing the great battle. He does not want to fight because he suspects that there is something wrong with killing (especially killing his own relatives and elders). "The flaw of pity," he says, "blights my very being; conflicting sacred duties confound my reason" (*Bhagavad Gita*, 2004, 859–860). This is the tragic problem of war: it involves a conflict of sacred duties. The god Krishna responds by claiming that Arjuna must "learn to endure fleeting things—they come and go." He goes on to tell Arjuna that individuality itself is unreal and that the individual's death has no significance. "He who thinks this self a killer and he who thinks it is killed both fail to understand; it does not kill, nor is it killed." While there are depths of Hindu philosophy to be plumbed here, the point fits quite well with our discussion of war as a public good that is indifferent to human individuality. On the battlefield, the ephemeral nature of life and death and individuality becomes obvious and tangible. The grind of war elicits the sublime experience of transcendence beyond attachment to the self. This insight can be liberating: indeed Indian thought is oriented around the project of seeing beyond the illusion of individuality and attachment to individual life.

Western traditions tend to view individuality as a serious good to be cherished and protected. From this perspective, the grind of war is dehumanizing. Even before the killing begins, individuals are combined together into the fighting unit. And war is directed at the homogeneous other. The enemy is viewed as an abstract entity identified by a proper noun: the Trojans, the Nazis, the Iraqis, and so on. Often these proper names degenerate into pejorative epithets: Krauts, Gooks, or Hajjis. Such names dehumanize by ignoring the moral differences among the individuals who make up the collective.

The Western just war tradition tries to rescue humanity by distinguishing between combatants and noncombatants. However, this distinction also dehumanizes, since it presumes that all combatants are the same: a uniformed soldier is a legitimate target, regardless of his private moral commitments, while noncombatants are protected, no matter how hateful and belligerent they are. In a recent book, Colonel Daniel Zupan has demonstrated how slippery the combatant/noncombatant distinction really is. Zupan asks us to consider the difficulty of distinguishing between a hateful, warmongering noncombatant and a peace-loving conscript. He concludes that we should give civilians the benefit of the doubt and treat them as noncombatants because "we cannot probe the depths of people's souls to see why they are working in a munitions factory" (Zupan, 2004, 88). This shows us the problem: war does not permit us to probe the depths of the souls of noncombatants or of combatants. But for the individual, it is the private depth of his soul that matters most.

The dehumanizing logic of war has long been noted. Simone Weil claimed in her memorable interpretation of the *Iliad* that the Greek epic is about that kind of abstract force that turns men into things. Most obviously, war turns living human bodies into corpses. But it also dehumanizes by turning men into functionaries of war. In wartime, the logic of war determines individual actions. There is no autonomy in war. Rather, private soldiers are units to be used by war. When one dies, another is inserted to replace it.

There is little room for moral choice in war. Individual soldiers cannot decide whether and how to fight. This is the aspect of war that makes it so difficult to talk about the morality of war. How can we apply morality to a situation in which free will is absent? It seems absurd to talk about responsibility in war or blame or even heroism—since the social mechanism of war does not allow much room for individual free choice. Indeed, this is why we strain to find heroic figures in war such as Tillman or Murphy. We long for an individual who, like Achilles, overcomes the grind and stands out among the crowd.

This grinding depersonalization is one aspect of what is so fascinating and even attractive about war. There is sublimity in giving yourself up to the mass. Responsibility and freedom are strenuous. Sometimes it is preferable to be lost in the crowd or to give up your attachment to individuality. Freud described this in terms of group narcissism. And the Hindu philosophers have described this as release from delusion. But we don't need Freudian theory or Hindu philosophy to acknowledge that there can be beauty in the movement of masses joining together in harmony. There is power in flowing with the crowd. And there is even a kind of rest that is found in losing individuality altogether in death. The daily struggle to keep the strands of our own individuality together in a coherent whole can be quite stressful. Sometimes we long for sleep or for intoxication or for destruction. This give us a hint about what happens in battle and in patriotic war fever, when individuals join with the masses and human beings come to embrace violence and destruction—a phenomenon described in detail recently by Chris Hedges. War leads individuals beyond themselves into a perspective in which it is possible to maintain, as Krishna does, that no one kills and nothing is killed.

MORALITY, POLITICS, AND BANALITY

If we follow Krishna into the grind of Ares, moral judgment becomes absurd. Morality takes the standpoint of individual conscience seriously. But deontological principles that demand respect for autonomy conflict with the general or public point of view that requires the state to uses masses of human beings for the greater good. Moral judgment focuses on choices that are to some degree free. Morality only makes sense in circumstances that allow for some degree of control.

Of course, we routinely apply moral judgment to public events and to political actions. We can describe states and statesmen as morally praiseworthy or as evil. Nazi Germany was evil. Hitler was evil. And the Holocaust was evil. It makes sense to speak in this way and to use the same term to describe both the statesman and the state. But this ordinary way of speaking can confuse us: Hitler's evil is different from the evil of the Nazi state. Hannah Arendt used the phrase, "the banality of evil," in her book *Eichmann in Jerusalem*, to describe the oddly impersonal evil of the state and its functionaries. To say that some thing is evil or virtuous, just or vile, we normally assume that the thing in question is a moral agent. And to be a moral agent, there must be a zone of privacy in which reflection, judgment, and moral choice take place.

Now the statesman does make free choices about how the assets of the state are to be used. But the state and its assets are more like objects—tools or weapons—that are used by the statesman. An "evil" state such as Nazi Germany is evil only insofar as the statesman uses the state and its assets for evil purposes. The phrase "assets of the state" includes everything that belongs to the state as an object or unit for use: the set of things that can be used by the authority who has the power of choice. Among these assets are the military, both its materiel and its soldiers. In war, soldiers are used as tools of the state. Thus, moral responsibility belongs to the statesman who makes decisions about how to use these tools.

Now a difficulty arises when we acknowledge that soldiers are not merely tools. They are human beings who do have the power of free choice and a private depth in which moral judgment takes place. They are agents. But the difficulty here is that a soldier's agency is strictly circumscribed by the requirements of military duty. Each individual soldier does have the power to make the choice whether to ship out or whether to pull the trigger. Conscientious objection or desertion are always options. We will return to this toward the end of the book. But the point here is that despite the depersonalizing demands of military service, soldiers are existentially free. The Stoics and the existentialists are right that we always retain the power to commit suicide. But beyond that sort of freedom, a soldier's power of choice and freedom are severely circumscribed. The average soldier does not deliberate about mission goals, strategies, or tactics. Rather, he is deployed as a unit. But this makes it difficult to focus a moral inquiry into war on the soldier. Rather, the focus of moral inquiry is on the statesmen, generals, and the constitutional system in which actual deliberation and decision making about war occurs. But at this general level of inquiry, the primary concern is the common good, not the needs, interests, and private concerns of the individual.

REALISM, PACIFISM, AND THE JUST WAR TRADITION

Those who think about the morality of war have long struggled to work through the tension between war as a public event and morality as focused on private conscience and individual responsibility. There are, broadly speaking, three possibilities for thinking about the morality of war: realism, pacifism, and the just war tradition.

Realists conclude that war is a public or historical movement and as such not easily amenable to the sorts of moral judgment that focus on individual intention and private conscience. Realists can cynically claim that the idea of morality in war is an oxymoron. Less cynical realism is grounded in utilitarianism. For the utilitarian, war should be about maximizing the greatest happiness for the greatest number. On this view, it is possible that some human beings can be sacrificed for the benefit of others.

Pacifism lies at the other end of the spectrum. Pacifists tend to retreat to the private sphere and hold that private conscience should trump utilitarian concerns. Pacifists will indeed opt out of military service via conscientious objection. This view tends to be deontological: pacifists will maintain that there is a higher duty to be obeyed, which trumps the utilitarian concern for the greater good.

Both approaches are persuasive. When one takes the view of the whole, individual deontological commitments can appear to be irrelevant to the task of serving the common good. But when one adopts the standpoint of individuality, it is difficult to see why a human being should ever kill or be killed in the name of an abstract entity like the state, especially if some other moral or religious duty prohibits such activities.

Between the two poles of realism and pacifism is the middle position known as the just war tradition. This tradition attempts to draw deontological limits around the basically utilitarian project of war. It is a compromise between a view that takes respect for individuality seriously and a utilitarian concern for the common good.

Just war ideas were developed by Stoics and Christians who held that there was a transcendent natural law toward which human beings were obliged even unto death. For Stoics and Christians, the ethical goal was to remain true to the moral law even in the face of loss, slavery, violence, and death. These moral traditions held that although war may grind your physical body into oblivion, there is a higher good beyond the physical body that should not (and on some interpretations *can* not) be surrendered to the grinder. For the Stoics and for Christians, there is a lasting kernel of virtue: the truly substantial good is the spiritual self, which is defined as that which transcends the vicissitudes of physical life. This personalist or individualist point of view resists the sort of de-individuation that we saw in Krishna's advice to Arjuna. The zone of personality and individuality can be described as a sort of "inner citadel" (see Hadot, 2001 and Berlin, 1969). In the modern world, this hardened redoubt of the self has been understood as the zone of privacy, the sphere of autonomy, or the stronghold of the conscience. Christians simply call it the soul. Western philosophy and religion tends to believe that there is an aspect of the self that is distinct from the public personae and social roles we inhabit. This private or autonomous self is supposed to resist the buffeting of fortune, including the grind of Ares. Hindu philosophy tells us that this is a sort of illusion. And war reminds us that in some circumstances, individuals can be used by the state for the greater good.

In war, individuals are asked to do things that would appear to violate the dictates of conscience. The justification of this violation of conscience is defined in terms that are primarily about collective goods. Augustine, the fourth century cleric, maintained that war should only be employed to bring about what George Weigel has called "the tranquility of order." The primary good to be defended by war is thus a public good. Moreover, individuals are not entitled to make war on their own. Rather, war is only justified as a political act. The just war tradition's ideas about legitimate authority make this clear: only those who have political legitimacy have the authority to declare war. Warriors only fight justly when they are viewed as servants or functionaries of the legitimate sovereign authority, whose duty is to protect the common good. The just war tradition does maintain that even within war, there are deontological limits: innocent noncombatants cannot be deliberately targeted, for example. But these limits are so broadly construed that innocents can be harmed as collateral damage.

The just war tradition reminds us of the basic ambivalence of human life. Human beings are pulled in various ways (and occasionally pulled apart) by these rival ways of understanding the self and its obligations. One way that this conflict has been described is by looking at the problem of "dirty hands." The conflict between moral (or private) and political (or public) goals appears to produce this problem: sometimes for the greater good we may have to do things that are immoral. Michael Walzer says that this conflict is typical of political action, since individuals can be used in defense of the common good (Walzer, 1973). Public officials must adopt the point of view of the collective and do their best to take account of the greater good. At some point they must bite the utilitarian bullet—and make decisions aimed to defend the public welfare, even if this requires using some individuals as tools.

Most people who talk about the ethics of war fail to acknowledge that the fact of dirty hands leaves us with a deeply disturbing sort of tension. The dialectical tension described here should disturb and disconcert us. In other words, we should feel dis-ease in thinking about war. The just war tradition is not a cure for this dis-ease. Rather, the just war ideal should remind us just how difficult it is to be good.

CONCLUSION

Most who think about war downplay the disturbance and tension of war. Pacifists claim that war is always wrong and that a person's main or only obligation is to conscience. They deny any value in war. But pacifists can be derided as free riders and hypocrites. It is easy enough to retreat to private conscience when others are defending the public order that makes this retreat possible. And it cannot be denied that war can produce virtue, while moving politics in a progressive direction. Like pacifists, utilitarian realists also overly simplify things. They claim that it is obvious that some individuals can be sacrificed for the common good. It is easy enough to believe this in the abstract—but it is more difficult to say this to the widows, orphans, and maimed soldiers who are produced by war—especially when the goods that are supposed to be produced by war are not entirely obvious.

The just war tradition is better, if it is interpreted in a way that recognizes the sublime dis-ease of war. Just war theory should not be understood as panacea that makes war easy to justify. The point of this book is to emphasize the complexity of war and the competing moral demands that make it difficult to think about the morality of war. War involves the direct killing of human beings. And one should never feel good about killing human beings—even when those we are killing are enemy combatants. As Colonel Zupan reminds us, killing in war is still an "instance of murder" (Zupan, 2004, 19). And yet, the killing of war does appear to be, in some circumstances, necessary for the common good. There is a conflict of values here that cannot be easily overcome.

CHAPTER TWO

THE WAR OF PUBLIC AND PRIVATE

War is the father of all and king of all . . .

Heraclitus

Heraclitus reminds us that "war is common and strife is just-ice, and all things happen according to strife and necessity" (DK22B80). Most of us do not like to admit this unhappy and ugly fact. Philosophers have always been troubled by inconsist-ency and conflict. Some have tried to will it away by postulating one principle or set of principles as superior to all others. Plato sought to resolve conflict by maintaining that there was one idea of good that united the plurality of goods. Christians argue that God unites the whole. And modern philosophers such as Kant and Mill have argued in favor of one primary moral principle or another. But there has never been consensus about moral prin-ciples. Indeed, if there were consensus, there would literally be no more war. If human beings agreed about values, not only would philosophers stop arguing among themselves but human beings would stop killing one another.

We must not be naïve in believing that we can eliminate conflict and war. We must continually work to ameliorate conflicts and limit war. The dream of pacifism—that war can be eradicated—is con-nected to the myth that just wars can be fought. Dreams and myths are useful: they remind us of our goals and aspirations. However, we must be careful not to mistake the dream for reality. The truth is that there will always be conflict. Not only do politicians disagree and people go to war but philosophers and religious adherents also fight among themselves. Even philosophers, such as Kant, who dream of peace recognize that war is a fact of life. Indeed, Kant claims that war is itself a means by which we will progress, after a long and ugly process, toward peace.

> Wars, tense and unremitting military preparations, and the resultant distress which every state must eventually feel within itself, even in the midst of peace—these are the means by which nature drives nations to make initially imperfect attempts, but finally after many devastations, upheavals and complete inner exhaustion of their powers, to take the step which reason could have suggested to them even without so many sad experiences. (Kant, 1991b, 47)

Kant seems to recognize Heraclitus' disturbing insight about the ubiquity of war. This view has been re-articulated by a variety of thinkers in the Western tradition, especially those who are called "Realists." In a sense, even Kant is a "realist": he recognizes the way that war serves as a sad but necessary mechanism for progress.[1] But Kant also hopes for peace, which he believes will develop through the spread of democracy and the creation of a cosmopolitan federation of peaceful nations. Kant's dream is a liberal-cosmopolitan order in which human autonomy is respected. The dream gives us something to strive for and a reason to believe that our striving will be successful. Kant holds individual autonomy as the primary good to be defended by the state. Another name for this in Kant's thought is "the kingdom of ends," which Kant describes as a systematic union of rational beings under common laws. In this ideal state, pursuit of the public good would be grounded in respect for private autonomy.

The realist alternative to Kantian liberalism holds that since war is ubiquitous, defense of the communal good is primary. In a world of war, short of the kingdom of ends, military power is necessary. And military power requires centralized political authority that is antithetical to liberal-democratic principles that place individual autonomy as the highest good. For the realist, public order trumps private autonomy. This collectivist approach can be identified in a variety of thinkers from Plato to Hegel. From Plato's perspective, the good of the polis is primary. And the good of the polis is actualized in a well-ordered state ruled by a central authority. Anything short of rule by a philosopher-king will result in anarchy, injustice, and war.

There are basically two choices here: we can centralize authority along Platonic lines; or we can work to disseminate democracy and liberal-cosmopolitan principles in hopes of fostering more rational behavior, as Kant advocated. The best solution we have settled upon so far is the Kantian approach. But this solution is a dream and a hope. There is no guarantee that we will achieve the dream of perpetual peace, because there will always be remaining conflicts in human life—as Heraclitus reminds us "war is common."

In contemporary discourse, the liberal or Kantian ideal is fleshed out in the idea of deliberative democracy grounded in fair procedural justice. The ideal of fair procedural justice is explained by John Rawls, who recognized that since conflict is unavoidable, the best solution is to establish fair procedures for resolving conflict. This does not eliminate conflict; rather it establishes conditions for resolution and amelioration. Stuart Hampshire has reiterated this point recently in his book, *Justice is Conflict* where he claims that conflict is "an essential and deep feature of human nature—both unavoidable and desirable—and rooted in our divergent imaginations and memories" (Hampshire, 2000, 37).

This helps to explain why war is inevitable. But it also makes it difficult to think about the morality of war. War results from conflict; and there are conflicting interpretations of the value of war. The depth of the problem is often explained in terms of the conflict among three basic ways of conceiving the morality of war: between pacifism, just war theory, and realism—as discussed in Chapter One.

War exposes, in an obvious and palpable way, the conflict between private conscience and public duty. For example, private individuals are not permitted to kill but public servants are. Indeed, state sanctioned killing is imbued with such value that soldiers become moral heroes. We reserve our highest praise for those who do things that would be considered barbarous and despicable if done in private life. The public/private distinction can help explain the tension between pacifists and defenders of war. Pacifists generally maintain that private morality is superior—and they don't like to make exceptions for the public necessity of killing. Defenders of war tend to hold that public order is primary—and they view killing simply as a means toward this end.

The conflict between public and private can be explained as a conflict between politics and morality. Politics has to do with life in the polis: it is about how groups of people organize their common life. Morality has to do with individual behavior, conscience, and the virtues and vices of private life. It is possible to apply morality to politics; and some argue that morality itself comes from a social contract or from historical conventions. But generally in this book I will use the term morality to describe private conscience as opposed to political or public goods. Moreover, I will consider morality as primarily "deontological": morality is focused on absolute duties such as are described by divine command, natural law, or Kantian ethics. Liberal thinkers, like Kant, place moral limits on politics: human rights are moral protections against state action. Opposed to this, public or political goods are best understood as utilitarian goods, such as were described by John Stuart Mill, where the goal is to maximize the greatest happiness for the greatest number, or to tend to the common good.

A BRIEF HISTORY OF CONFLICTING VIEWS OF WAR

Tensions in thinking about morality, politics, and war can be seen in both main sources of the Western tradition: in the Judeo-Christian religious tradition and in the Greek philosophical tradition.

Jesus tells us to love our enemies and to avoid returning evil for evil (see Fiala, 2007). Jesus advocates a kind of pacifism that turns away from political power. Unfortunately, love and pacifism could not prevent Jesus' crucifixion. The fact that Jesus was executed by the political authorities is a reminder of the way that private individuals can be sacrificed by political authorities for the greater good. The Romans believed that it was necessary to destroy and dismantle Judaism—an approach that culminated in the destruction of the temple in Jerusalem in 70 AD. As a response, the Jesus movement was initially opposed to political power—since political power was viewed as a threat to private piety and the ethic of love.

At the same time, Paul tells us (in chapter 13 of *Romans*) that the sovereign employs the sword to execute God's wrath on wrongdoers. This appears to justify the sovereign's decision to take up weapons against enemies. Early Christians such as Augustine wrestled with the question of whether Christians should serve in the military and with the question of how love can be connected to political power. This question became especially pressing after Constantine converted the Empire to Christianity. The tension between peace, love, justice, and political power eventually resulted in the difficult compromise position that we know as the just war tradition. The just war ideal reminds us that there are rare occasions when individual lives can be destroyed for the good of the whole. This view develops from out of a recognition of the tensions and contradictions of human life. For Augustine, the demands of the City of God stand in contrast to the realities of the City of Man. According to Augustine, we live in a second-best world. In the best world, there would be no need to kill. But in our fallen world, war is an inevitable, albeit mournful, fact of life necessitated by love and duty: the duty of loving our neighbors means that unfortunately sometimes it is our duty to kill in defense of the innocent.

This sort of tension between public and private goods can also be found in the Greek tradition. Plato and the Greek poets knew that we live in an imperfect and tragic state. In his later dialogue, the *Laws*, Plato gives upon the utopian dream of his *Republic*. He concludes in the *Laws* that we must make do with a second-best world. In the best world, philosophers would rule and Socrates would not have been executed. But in our second-best world, we see the conflict between public and private fleshed out in the life and death of Socrates—in a way that is parallel to the life and death of Jesus. Socrates was a noble servant of the state and a brave soldier. But his refusal to silence his private conscience led to his destruction at the hands of the political authorities. Socrates was praised by Alcibiades (in the *Symposium*) as a courageous warrior—an important point since Alcibiades himself was an important general in the Peloponnesian War (and, it should be noted, a general who betrayed Athens). Not only does Alcibiades praise Socrates for his military service, but we know that Socrates willingly submitted to the will of the state—even obeying the order to drink the hemlock. Despite his service to the polis, Socrates is also looked to as a model of individual conscience—the gadfly of conscience. Socrates refused to commit injustice and he refused to shut his mouth in deference to public authority—even when this would have saved his own life.

The Greek poets also saw the tension between obedience and individuality. Achilles retreated into the isolation of his own camp, deserting his comrades while he brooded in private over a personal injustice. And indeed, Achilles remained concerned primarily with his own private values. His return to battle is not motivated by concern for the well-being of the Greeks or with obedience to Agamemnon; rather he fights to avenge his friend Patroclus and to pursue personal glory.

The ancient Hebrew tradition contains similar stories of the tension between obedience and individual conscience. Recall, for example, Saul's refusal to commit an atrocity commanded by God. Samuel, the prophet of God, had commanded that Saul should massacre all of the Amalekites including all the men, women, children, and animals. But Saul spared some of the enemy. And Saul was then condemned by Samuel for his reluctance to commit omnicide. According to Samuel, atrocity was required by God's command. Saul disobeyed God and subsituted his own moral judgment for the commands of the prophet. In the Hebrew tradition, the model of piety, faith, and obedience is Abraham. But Abraham's faith led him to be willing to kill his own beloved son. For modern readers of these stories, Abraham may appear as a madman, whose faith leads him to sacrifice that which he loves best; and Saul appears, perhaps, to be the more reasonable individual. But the tradition praises Abraham and condemns Saul. The question that these stories raise is the degree to which private conscience (and private faith) should guide our actions. In the Greek tradition, the dialogue with Crito shows us a similar sort of question, with Socrates deciding that he should subordinate himself to the will of the state.

Similar conflicts have recurred throughout history. Philosophers such as Machiavelli, Leibniz, Locke, Kant, Fichte, Hegel, Emerson, Thoreau, and Marx had to reconcile—each in their own way—the tension between private conscience and public life (see Fiala, 2002b). In the twentieth century, philosophers such as James, Addams, Royce, Russell, Heidegger, and Dewey struggled with the same problem of whether and how to address political power.

We also see this sort of conflict today—between obedience to a higher authority and remaining true to your conscience. Consider, for example, soldiers such as the American Army Lieutenant Ehren Watada, who have refused to be deployed to Iraq. These individuals volunteered to serve in the military but then decided that the war they were being asked to fight was not just. Such stories—from Jesus, Saul, and Socrates to these contemporary cases—leave us wondering about the tragic conflict between morality and politics, between public good and private conscience.

Kings and generals, soldiers and presidents appear to have to set private conscience aside in order to work for the greater good. The motto of service may be found in Tennyson's lines: "Theirs not to make reply, theirs not to reason why, theirs but to do and die." Indeed, great warriors are celebrated for sacrificing themselves for public goods. Even when the battles in which they die are ill-advised or unjust, there is still something noble in such sacrifice. History is full of praise for the self-sacrificial soldier. And we continue to praise those who sacrifice their lives and their consciences for the public good. Individual warriors fight for a variety of reasons—some personal and some political. Some are conscripted, others are born into the profession, and in our modern democracies, soldiers are hired as professionals. But once enlisted as a soldier, the warrior becomes a functionary of the state, an asset to be deployed by the state in defense of public goods. Warriors are praised for virtues such as loyalty, fidelity, and obedience. The Marine Corps motto, "semper fidelis," is an obvious example of the warrior's virtues.

Loyalty, fidelity, and obedience can appear to be old-fashioned values that do not fit well within a modern liberal scheme of values. And philosophers have continually warned us against unquestioning obedience to authority. In traditional societies—in ancient Greece or Israel—it was easy to accept the subordination of the individual to the state as natural and inevitable. Indeed, military service was often seen as a religious duty; and in a hierarchical culture it is presumed that some individuals are to be used by others in defense of the whole. Jesus and Socrates each sacrificed themselves for the good of the whole in this way, even as they advocated—each in his own way—that private conscience, piety, and faith are higher than the goods of political life.

WAR AND RAISON D'ETAT

Thankfully, most of us no longer believe that prophets such as Samuel have the divine power to command omnicidal warfare. Although we expect the military to operate according to a model of faithful service, modern democratic political life is not based upon divine imprimatur. Thus, in a secular world without kings or prophets, it is not so easy to resolve the tension between public and private. It may have been easier to remain loyal and faithful when it was widely believed that divine Providence ruled over social life.

But the genocides and atrocities of the twentieth century make it harder to believe that political power is always benevolently and providentially employed.

War is a blunt instrument of social change that inevitably kills innocent persons and uses soldiers as means without respect for their autonomy. The modern problem is whether it is possible for liberals committed to deontological moral principles to justify war and its inevitable violations of human rights. This is done by focusing on war as a public good and downplaying the significance of individual losses in war.

It is possible thus to explain away the tension between public and private in war. Soldiers do, after all, voluntarily join the military—at least this is true today in most Western democratic nations. But once they sign up, it seems that they must do their duty, even if they disagree with the wars they are being asked to fight. Similarly, the just war theory can explain away civilian casualties by calling it "collateral damage" and by using the "doctrine of double effect": civilian casualties are permitted so long as they are not directly intended. But this explanation still looks like a violation of individual rights from the standpoint of the noncombatants who are killed.

There is considerable tension between the point of view of the individual and the point of view of the collective, tension between the perspective of private life and the perspective of the public good. This conflict is deeply tragic: a serious conflict of important goods. On the one hand, we value the private good of individual conscience and life, on the other, we esteem the public good of the state or the whole. In defense of the public good it can appear necessary to violate the rights of individuals. In the war on terrorism, to cite our most recent example, terror suspects have been detained without habeas corpus rights, abused, and even tortured. All of this may, of course, be easily justified from a standpoint that takes public goods as primary. If torture and indefinite detention prevent terrorism, then they serve the public good. But this public good will never fully compensate individuals for violations of their rights. Soldiers are permanently damaged, torture victims will remain scarred, and civilians who are killed and maimed can never be healed, even if war produces public good.

War is ultimately about mass nouns—troops, armies, peoples, and the public good. Individuals only matter within war as members of these collectives. One way of resolving this tension is to emphasize the fact that war is a public event of world-historical significance. Hegel exemplifies this point of view: he claimed that war reminds us that individuality is fleeting while also showing us that states and historical movements are more real and lasting. State-centered theories will claim that we need to overcome squeamishness about individual loses in war and focus on the majesty of the state. Utilitarians will argue that private attachments need to be reordered and reconceived from the standpoint of the greater happiness principles. Indeed, realists will argue that we often need to do some pretty horrible things for the greater good. But such are *les raisons d'etat*. Even if we don't go so far as to affirm utilitarianism and realism, many appear to think that qualms about war are supposed to be kept to oneself and only expressed in private. Some may believe that during wartime, dissent is tantamount to treason. And many would agree that soldiers should not question the wars they are asked to fight. The standard view seems to be that conscience is a private affair that should not interfere with public duty, especially in time of war.

Conscience is an individual's soft, quiet, inner voice that asks moral questions late into the night. But war is a raging clamor organized by those at the top of the political hierarchy. War is oriented toward collective goods that most individuals cannot see or understand. There is no time or space in war for individual conscience. The movements of men and the clash of weapons drown out this soft quiet voice and reasons of state trump individual interests, ideas, and moral judgments.

Most thinkers in the Western tradition prior to the seventeenth and eighteenth centuries tended to affirm the power and the authority of the public sphere, as if there were wisdom in the din of war and virtue in the busy-ness of public life. Most of us continue to believe in the state and its concern for the public good. Despite our doubts, we tend to grit our teeth and go along with *raison d'etat*. In public we are utilitarian—focused on public goods and maximizing happiness for the greatest number. From the point of view of the collective, individuals are replaceable and expendable: we can each be sacrificed to the whole. This extends even to the ruler. Machiavelli, for example, argued that the prince must be prepared to sacrifice private morality and individual conscience for the good of the whole. "A ruler who wishes to maintain his power must be prepared to act immorally when this becomes necessary" (Machiavelli, 1988, chapter XV, 55). This means, at its most extreme, that the ruler must be prepared to go to hell in defense of the common good. If this is true, then it is no wonder that the ruler can order his subjects or citizens to violate their private moral scruples.

But a rival trend defends private morality and individual conscience against the demands of public good. Socrates and Jesus each in their own way refused to entirely subordinate private conscience for public good. Jesus said (Mat. 22.21), "Render unto Caesar the things which are Caesar's, and unto God the things that are God's." Christian pacifists such as John Howard Yoder and Stanley Hauerwas tend to agree with Tertullian and view military service as a sort of idolatry that places allegiance to the state above faith in God. Private conscience is extolled in the philosophical tradition as well. In his *Apology*, Socrates claimed that out of obedience to God he would never give up his effort to be the gadfly of conscience and he maintained that he would never obey an unjust order.

But it is not until the seventeenth and eighteenth centuries that private individuality becomes the central value. Descartes begins his philosophizing with the ego. Locke claims that individuals have a right to revolt against an unjust state. And Kant claims that individuals should not be used as a means for a further end. These sorts of ideas tend toward pacifism. Emerson's post-Kantian ideal of self-reliance is, for example, transformed by Thoreau in his essay on "Civil Disobedience" into an antiwar ideal. Thoreau's ideas are taken up by Tolstoy, Gandhi, and Martin Luther King Jr. In his "Letter from Birmingham Jail," King connects his own pacifism and civil disobedience to Jesus, Socrates, and the basic idea that individual conscience is in a sense higher than the state and its status quo. And in his antiwar sermon, "Beyond Vietnam," King argues that silence is betrayal. King's basic point is that by subordinating individual conscience to political power and the momentum of the status quo, we tacitly permit injustice to persist.

The difficulty of defending private conscience as the only value in life is, of course, the fact that it is public order that allows private conscience to flourish. Defenders of the just war theory recognize this fact. Individual liberty is protected by the state. Thus, a threat to the public good of sovereignty is conceived as a threat to individual liberty and private conscience. And when individual liberty is threatened—as it is, for example, by terrorism, aggression, or by a corrupt and oppressive regime—then it may be necessary to revert to the view of the whole and fight a war that violates individual liberty as a way of protecting it. Just war theorists emphasize the public good of security or what Augustine has called the tranquility of order. Some individuals may have to sacrifice their rights—including liberty and life—in order to establish security and the tranquility of order.

This should sound like an unfortunate and even contradictory compromise. My purpose here is to indicate these sorts of contradictions and the tension produced by the difference between public and private goods. There will always be a conflict between the common good and individual conscience. War is the most obvious and most difficult manifestation of this tragic conflict.

MODELS OF THE CONFLICT

There are very few defenders of absolute individualism. Only the most ardent anarchists and libertarians will claim that individuals can never be used by the state. Grudging acquiescence to the state has a long lineage that goes back to Jesus, Socrates, and the Stoics. Jesus willingly sacrificed himself for his followers and acquiesced to both Pilate and the Jewish authorities who condemned him. Like Socrates, Jesus could have run away or staged a revolution. But defenders of private conscience tend to believe that if it is wrong for the state to use individuals, then it is also wrong for individuals to rise up against the state in violence, if such violence will harm other individuals. Pacifism appears to fit especially well with the idea that individuals should *not* be used or abused in pursuit of power: but pacifism thus leaves the individual without any violent resort against an abusive and oppressive state. The hope of pacifists and nonviolent activists from Gandhi to King is that the example of individual virtue and the private discipline of nonviolence will have an impact on public policy.

We see a similar sort of self-sacrifice in the model of Socrates. Socrates famously refused to leave Athens, despite the fact that Athens had betrayed him. In the *Crito*, he has an imaginary conversation with the Laws of Athens. The Laws argue that they have sustained him and that Socrates owes allegiance to Athens as a result. But the fact of the matter is that Athens was not just. Athens had recently emerged from a war in which it had behaved badly and the political turmoil in Athens included several purges and other assaults against justice. The last straw might have been the very trial of Socrates, when democracy made its most famous mistake: the assembly voted to condemn a just man. But Socrates—according to Plato's interpretation—refused to leave, believing that allegiance was owed to a state that had proved itself to be immoral and corrupt.

Another exemplary source for the tragic conflict between individual conscience and public good is found in the Stoics. Stoicism emphasizes the freedom of the rational and virtuous person. But this freedom is limited, since the Stoics also emphasized obedience to the state and to destiny. The Stoic is willing to die in service. And, like Socrates, the Stoic is willing to commit suicide rather than to violate the public order. The model for Stoicism is the soldier who obeys, even unto death. This sort of obedience is grounded in faith that the public order is guided by Providence. The individual should not protest against destiny or the state—since this destiny serves a purpose that transcends his own private concerns. Seneca puts it this way, in his essay "On Providence": "it is to the common interest for the best men to be soldiers, so to speak, and do our service" (Seneca, 1958, 40–41). He continues: "the best men are conscripts of toil."

Socrates and the Stoics thus hold that the individual should submit to the state and that private conscience can be overridden by the demands of public necessity. To be clear, we must note that Socrates and the Stoics did not claim that the private conscience should completely submit to public necessity. Socrates claimed that he would continue to be a philosophical gadfly to the state. Indeed, he claimed that the state benefited from the critical questioning of the private individual. But at the end of the day, Socrates was willing to submit to death—like the good soldier he was—rather than to disobey. There are deep and well-argued ideas that ground this sort of obedience. Plato was worried that anarchy would result if individuals were empowered to follow their private inclinations. But this call for obedience and submission appears to be antithetical to the ideals of democracy. Indeed, in the *Republic*, Plato actually argues that democracy and individualism are dangerous.

Modern liberal-democratic politics, following Locke, rejects the Platonic view by maintaining that the state should respect private conscience. Modern individualism places private conscience above public conformity. The heroes of modern democracy are individuals like Jefferson, Thoreau, and King, who argued that private conscience should lead to actions aimed at revolutionizing the state. The heroes of democracy were not content to "argue but obey" as Kant once put it. Rather, they argued and resisted—or at least argued and disobeyed. And their disobedience and resistance was designed to make the state more moral.

Nonetheless, most of us tend to think that in war, reasons of state trump the moral scruples of private conscience. One reason for this is that war is the most public of events. Individuals do not wage war, states do. In war, the state uses individuals as a means to its larger ends. And war is ultimately a public endeavor that aims at the greater good. The language of the just war theory speaks of just causes for war. But justice in going to war is understood primarily in terms of the collective good of defending sovereignty against the crime of aggression. Even humanitarian interventions—which aim to defend individuals against injustice—are public events that must focus on collective security, even at the expense of the rights of some of the individuals caught up in the war.

CONCLUSION

Since Heraclitus, it has been obvious that life consists of conflicts of values and identities. Although individuals themselves can be internally conflicted about things, the most dangerous and destructive conflicts are those between individuals and groups of individuals. Most individuals want to be left alone to worship, play, love, and work. And yet, it does seem that national boundaries and sovereignty matters. We do identify with the whole—and describe ourselves as Americans or as Iraqis or what have you. But these collective identifications are tenuous and are often the fictions of what Benedict Anderson once called "imagined communities." Some Americans view themselves as Southerners or Hawaiians or Navajos first. Others take their religious affiliation as the only thing that matters—the Amish, for example. And in some "nations," national identity is almost nonexistent: Iraq consists of tribes, religious rivalries, and ethnic divisions—Kurds, Sunnis, Shiites, etc.

The frontier, as it were, of the struggle between private conscience and public authority is found in war because war requires us to take seriously those collective identifications that are, in times of peace, often ignored as we pursue our private vision of the good.

NOTE

1. For Realist interpretations of Kant see Wagner, 2007 or Waltz, 1962. For a Liberal interpretation see Doyle, 1997.

CHAPTER THREE

PLATO'S PROPHECY AND KANT'S DREAM

Our guardian is soldier and philosopher in one.

Plato, Republic *(525b)*

One could argue that war is the primary subject of political philosophy. At least, war is always about politics. And massive political changes are usually the result of war. War is widespread political violence oriented around public goods, such as territorial control and governance. Clausewitz famously put it this way: "war is the continuation of politics by other means" (Clausewitz, 1982, 119). Clausewitz's study of war indicates that the political or public nature of war should never be forgotten. War is primarily about political power and the public good of defending the collective well-being of the people, including—in the case of democracies—their individual rights.

There have been two primary ways for dealing with the problem of war and politics: a Platonic approach and a Kantian approach. The Platonic approach calls for centralized government with strong guardians selected to defend the state against the inevitability of war. Some interpreters of Plato argue that he remains a democrat (Recco, 2007), while others see in Plato a form of totalitarianism (Popper, 1971). The traditional view claims that Plato's proposed political ideal is rule by a philosopher-king. The Platonic approach is less concerned with individual autonomy and private conscience than with the good of the whole. The dream of a philosopher-king who would rule the whole is, however, haunted by Plato's prophetic insight that even the best polis will devolve under the pressures of strife and war toward democracy and then from democracy to an unjust tyranny. Plato's prophecy is that political life is unstable and will be haunted by the specter of war.

In his farewell address at West Point, General Douglas MacArthur invoked Plato to describe the need for military virtue. MacArthur said, "the soldier above all other people prays for peace, for he must suffer and bear the deepest wounds and scars of war. But always in our ears ring the ominous words of Plato, that wisest of all philosophers: 'Only the dead have seen the end of war.'" This direct quote cannot be found in Plato—but it is found in the writing of American philosopher George Santayana, offered as a response to Woodrow Wilson's idea of a war to end all wars (Santayana, 1937, vol. 9, 97). Santayana thinks that the dream of perpetual peace is naïve. And Plato would have agreed. According to Plato, any state that is not ruled by centralized power concentrated in the hands of a philosopher-king is at risk of war—both internal and external. Since there are no states ruled by philosopher-kings, the conclusion is that conflict will never end. From the Platonic perspective, the state must remain prepared for war; and individuals—including the philosopher-king—must be willing to sacrifice themselves for the greater good of the polis.

Kant's approach calls for greater respect for autonomy and it hopes for a world beyond war. The hope of perpetual peace is, from Kant's perspective, intimately linked to the spread of democracy and greater respect for individual autonomy. Despite the fact that Kant recognizes the sublimity of war (as discussed in Chapter One), Kant viewed war as a "scourge of the human race" that should be eliminated (Kant, 1998b, 57 footnote). Plato thought that war would continually require individuals to sacrifice themselves for the state and generally viewed this as an opportunity for individuals to develop virtue. Kant hoped that respect for individual autonomy would spell the end of war, while also noting that war "creates more evil men than it takes away" (ibid.). Kant was not naïve enough to suppose that war would end in his own lifetime—but he dreamed of a future in which it would. Indeed, Kant argued that there was a moral imperative to hope that society could be improved, that autonomy could be respected, and that a cosmopolitan peace could be created. In short, Kant maintained that hope for the "kingdom of ends" was a morally necessary, regulative ideal.

Kant recognized that human beings are ambivalent, plagued by a sort of "unsocial sociability" that drives us together while also driving us apart (Kant, 1991b, 44). The dream of perpetual peace is a normative ideal that is aimed at solving the disturbance created by this ambivalence: we must hope for a world beyond war, even though our unsocial nature leads us into conflict. Indeed, for Kant, war is itself the mechanism that will help propel us toward this dream. Kant thought that the barbarity of warfare would eventually lead enlightened people to develop republican political arrangements and a peaceful federation of nations. While Plato thought that war and conflict would produce continual political instability, Kant hoped that through war, peace would emerge.

PLATO'S PROPHECY

According to Plato, justice is the proper organization of the parts of society. Proper organization is needed because the parts of society are at war with one another. Even within the individual, there is war, since the parts of the soul are in conflict with one another. The solution to war is wise central organization.

For an Athenian of Plato's generation, war was a ubiquitous fact of life (see Frank, 2007 and Baracchi, 2002). Plato's *Republic* addresses an audience that shared the sorts of concerns that we see in other works of the time, such as Aristophanes' comedies *Lysistrata* and *Peace* or Thucydides' *History of the Peloponnesian War*. War, conflict, and injustice lead to the sort of inquiry that Plato recounts in the *Republic*. For the Athenians, the problem was how to deal with the imperial hubris, injustice, and factional strife that led to the loss of the Peloponnesian War. Plato's discussion of justice in the *Republic* revolves around these sorts of questions. The dialogue is supposed to occur at some point during the war. And the concluding myth tells of Er, "a warrior bold," whose body was left on the battlefield for 10 days among the rotting and decaying corpses. The main characters in the dialogue were involved in the war. Indeed, like Socrates, they have the names of warriors: Socrates literally means "Sure-Strength" (see Craig, 1994). Polemarchus (literally "War Ruler") and his father Cephalus made their fortunes supplying arms to the Athenians during the war. It turns out that Polemarchus and his friend Niceratus ("Victory") were eventually executed by the Thirty Tyrants. The famous discussion of justice in Book 1 finds Thrasymachus ("Bold Fighter") defining justice as doing good to friends and harm to enemies. This definition helps to explain the basic point of view during war: we help our friends and kill our enemies. Socrates reminds us that it is difficult to figure out who our friends and enemies are and what they actually deserve. This makes sense if we recall that one of Socrates' pupils and friends, Alcibiades, was a general whose betrayals eventually cost Athens victory in the war.

Plato's proposed solution for the problem of justice is the pursuit of wisdom. Socrates contends in the heart of the *Republic*, that the best guardian would be a soldier and philosopher in one (*Republic* 525b). Not only does the ruler need to be good at warfare, he also needs to be wise and virtuous. A virtuous ruler and his army will fight well and wisely. And these same virtues will serve to eliminate strife within the polis itself. Indeed, Plato also seemed to think that philosophers themselves also needed to be good at warfare—as Socrates himself was—because warrior virtues are useful for the polemics of philosophical dialogue.

Plato saw strife and war within the polis, in the clash of factions within the city. Plato also holds that there is "division and strife" in the soul because we hold contrary opinions about things (*Republic* 604c–d). The solution is to put wisdom and virtue in charge, whether in the city or in the soul. The goal of justice is to construct a rational division of labor that would eliminate strife among the parts.

The cure for war within the city is the philosopher-king, who will be authorized to use whatever means are necessary—including lies, manipulation, and eugenics—to forge a stable and just society. On this view, peace is to be instituted by the philosopher-king. But until a wise soldier-king takes charge, the city will be plagued by war and factionalism. This leads Plato to describe a process of degeneration through less-perfect forms of social organization. For Plato, democracy is nearly the worst form of government, because democratic people lack self-control and moderation. One of the problems for democracy is that it gives people the liberty (or license) to choose whether or not they want to go to war (*Republic* 557e). For Plato, this is absurd: the generals should control war-making and the private soldiers should obey.

Now this sort of liberty of the private individual will be exactly what liberals such as Kant will extol as both a necessary feature of morality—respect for individual liberty—and as an antidote to war. But Plato brings this idea up only to mock it. Plato says that democracy sounds like a desirable and pleasant state of affairs.

But it is not. Plato prophesied that democracy would lead to the destruction of the state, as democratic people will elect a tyrant who would rule unjustly. The tyrant would also stir up faction at home and war abroad in order to consolidate power. "He is always stirring up some war so that the people may be in need of a leader . . . and also that being impoverished by war taxes they may have to devote themselves to their daily business and be less likely to plot against him" (*Republic* 566e). The tyrant would thus exploit the anarchy of democracy and take over, using war as a pretext and a means to consolidate power.

Plato's prophecy was that democracy would devolve into faction and war, while war would spell the end of democracy. The solution is a strong central authority who can organize society justly. But for Plato, the philosopher-king appears to be a dream and the unjust tyrant a more likely outcome. Democracy is at risk of its own overthrow, especially when war can be used by a tyrant to gain power. There are two levels of this prophecy. Plato focused primarily on faction and war within the polis. But at the level of international affairs, the same problem exists: that without a strong and just sovereign ruling over diverse political entities, there will be war. The international problem is best described by Hobbes two millennia later. Hobbes seems to agree with Plato that war and conflict are natural and that a strong central authority is necessary to preserve the peace.

KANT'S DREAM

In the Enlightenment, Kant and others dreamed of perpetual peace. This dream was closely connected with hope for the dawning of an era of enlightenment that would include both philosophical progress and the spread of liberal democracy. As liberal democracy spread around the world and science supplanted superstition, war would end and cosmos would develop out of chaos. Kant thought that war was itself the mechanism that would eventually lead to the creation of the solution: at some point, through exhaustion and ubiquitous destruction, men would realize that democracy and a federation of nations was the solution to the problem of war (Kant, 1991b).

This is very similar to Hegel's idea of the end of history: history was a struggle of political ideas that ends with the dawning of the enlightenment ideal of liberal democracy. Although Hegel is notorious for proclaiming "the end of history," he recognized that it would still take long centuries for liberal democracy to take hold. In the meantime, there would be war. The difficulty with Hegel's thinking about war and politics is that Hegel's ideas remain mired in a collectivist model: the vantage point of history looks at wars and states from a perspective that downplays the moral depth of individual life. This point of view has much in common with a Platonic conception of the state as an organic whole in which social organization is key; and in which individuals—guardians and even philosophers—have an obligation to sacrifice themselves for the whole.

Kant provides us with a deeper sense of individuality than Hegel did. Kant's deontological moral theory is an argument in favor of the inviolability of the individual. Indeed, it is significant that Kant's defense of individualism is related to his understanding of the way that war is rooted in our "unsocial sociability." Kant tells us that man not only has a tendency to "live in society" but also that he has "a greater tendency to live as an individual, to isolate himself, since he also encounters in himself the unsocial characteristic of wanting to direct everything in accordance with his own ideas" (Kant, 1991b, 44).

The idea of directing things according to our own ideas is a way of describing autonomy: autonomy means to be a lawgiver for yourself. For Kant, it is autonomy that gives human beings a kind of sacred or absolute value. Even in times of war, Kant held that the state cannot simply use individuals as a means. This is why Kant held that citizens must be given the power to consent to wars. When liberal democracy finally spreads, Kant hoped that there would be no more war because rational individuals would not consent to the sorts of violations of liberty that are required by war. In a sense, then, our individualistic and antisocial tendency is both the cause of war and its solution. Individualism causes war insofar as we isolate ourselves in antagonism against others; individualism ends war when autonomy is respected in the republican constitution.

Of course, since Kant and Hegel, there have been numerous wars. But theorists continue to dream Kant's dream. Francis Fukuyama's claims about the end of history provide one example: Fukuyama agreed with Hegel and Kant that history (and war) would end with the dawn of a liberal era. Fukuyama once thought that this new post-historical era was occurring with the end of the Cold War. After Fukuyama, Michael Doyle claimed that Kant's thesis about the connection between liberal democracy and peace provides a basic rule of history: according to Doyle, it is true that liberal democracies do not go to war against one another. This thesis has been adopted by John Rawls whose later work continues to dream the Kantian dream of an international order governed by what he calls the "Law of Peoples." The 1990s were a time of optimism about history and about the prospects for perpetual peace.

CONTINUING CONFLICTS

But this optimism changed after September 11, 2001. It seemed that history had not ended and that prospects were haunted by what Samuel Huntington called a "clash of civilizations." Indeed Fukuyama gave a lecture in 2002 that asked the question: "Has History Started Again?" In this lecture, Fukuyama reassesses the Kantian dream. He makes it clear that we are confronted by a choice of alternatives that have to do with a conflict between liberal internationalism and national sovereignty. On the one hand, the Kantian dream is that wars will diminish when there is democracy at the international level. On the other hand, the ideal of national sovereignty seems to impose a limit for the development of liberal internationalism. Liberal internationalism updates the Kantian dream to include equality of representation across international borders. The dream of perpetual peace is tied to this idea of a global system in which "peoples" (to use Rawls' language) are adequately recognized. The difficulty of this dream is that nations that are more powerful will not want to give up their power in order to achieve the dream of equality of representation. We can see this conflict enacted in the United Nations, for example, in the fact that there are inequities regarding which nations are permanent members of the Security Council. In addition to this institutional disparity, the United States has shown its unwillingness to participate cooperatively on the international scene. In addition to the unilateral invasion of Iraq in 2003, the United States has flouted international conventions against torture and the rights of prisoners, it has refused to support international institutions such as the World Court, and it has refused to act cooperatively to solve the problem of Global Climate Change.

We are thus at a crossroads for thinking about war and peace. On the one hand, we value private conscience and we hold the individual human person to have absolute worth and inherent dignity. On the other hand, we still think in terms of states, public authority, and power politics. This clash is inevitable, as it replicates the conflict between deontological ethics and utilitarianism: sometimes we value individuals as ends-in-themselves but at other times we recognize that the demands of the greater good can ask individuals to sacrifice their liberty and their lives for the general welfare. Sometimes the greater good of humankind is a priority. But at other times, national sovereignty is the primary good, grounded in the right to self-governance.

The war on terrorism has made these sorts of conflicts clear. Terrorism challenges liberal democracies in two ways. The direct threat is obvious: terrorists target citizens in a systematically unsystematic way in order to disrupt stability. The more insidious threat is that liberal democracies will react to terrorism in ways that will violate the very principles upon which they are based—violating civil liberties, flirting with torture, and employing mass violence in an effort to hunt down the individual purveyors of terror. Reactions to the September 11 attacks in the "war on terrorism" show us that this indirect threat is very real. Our open society has changed its structure in order to prevent terrorists from taking advantage of this very openness. And the war on terror has used tactics that violate traditional just war thinking. At issue here is not only increased security and surveillance but also the preventive use of military force, the use of secret courts, extraordinary prisons, and torture. Defenders of such tactics claim that our thinking about justice, law, and war needs to change in order to accommodate new threats. What is remarkable is that citizens have generally approved of most of the tactics used in the war on terrorism. It is not too much to conclude that fear can motivate democratic citizens to support policies that subvert democratic principles.

This problem is not new. According to Hobbes, fear of war motivated individuals to sacrifice their natural rights in order to create the Leviathan. Indeed, the problem can be traced back to the Greeks. Democracy suffered and brutality flourished in ancient Athens during the turmoil created by the Peloponnesian war. In the *Republic*, Plato noted that the volatile nature of democracies is related to the tendency of citizens to react without virtue. Plato

claimed that democracies will fall as a result of citizens' suscept-
ibility to passions such as fear, hatred, and indolence. This problem
has been, for the most part, ignored by modern defenders of liberal
democracy from Locke to Fukuyama. Such thinkers argue that
liberal democracy represents the most stable form of government
because it satisfies the desire of citizens to have their basic human
rights respected. Kant's dream was that democracy will produce
perpetual peace because citizens would be unwilling to sacrifice
their happiness to fight a war; but this is also tied to the idea that
citizens would be unwilling to sacrifice their liberty (and would
be unwilling to violate the liberty of others) in order to preserve
security in light of threats—whether real or imagined. The war on
terror appears to call this dream into question by showing us that
democratic citizens are susceptible to warlike passions and the lure
of the mob; we want security and we are willing to accept means
that appear immoral to obtain it. Recent events should thus direct
our attention back to Plato's prophecy—the threat of insecurity can
stimulate a retreat to collectivism that results in behavior that is
immoral and illiberal. At the very least, recent events show us that
a minimal effort on the part of a small group of terrorists can create
a large negative impact on democratic institutions.

CONCLUSION

When Plato considered democracy, he had in mind, primarily, a
form of government that ruled according to the opinions of the
masses. The war on terrorism shows us that Plato was right about
the fact that demagogues can easily manipulate the passions and
opinions of the masses. Thus, we might think that democracy is
not the best form of government for obtaining peace and justice:
it is too easy for leaders to whip up war frenzy. The form of government dreamed of by Kant shows us an antidote to this problem
of democracy. Kant advocated a liberal republic in which persons
are respected as having basic human rights but in which public
opinion is not the only guide to policy decisions. Kant's ideal is
similar to what Aristotle and Cicero called "mixed government"
(a mix of various forms of rule). However, even this modified form
of democracy brings with it the same risks. After all, the United
States is best described as a republic with close affinities to the ideal
Kant imagined—but American foreign policy is not perfect and the

American people are susceptible to demagoguery. Kant thought that "publicity" (freedom of speech and openness on the part of government) would be the key to ending war and injustice. But the war on terrorism has shown us the limits of the idea of publicity as a brake on injustice: the government can invoke public safety concerns in order to control information and manipulate the public sphere to serve the interests of power. Even a new administration in Washington has not changed this: President Obama has resisted releasing graphic evidence of torture and prisoner abuses in the war on terrorism, based on concerns for public safety.

The solution is more and better citizenship. Plato worried that democratic individuals would pursue self-interest at the expense of the state because they would not be able to rule themselves according to wisdom and justice. If we presume that most citizens are morally and intellectually corrupt, then Plato would appear to be correct. The tendency of selfish and shortsighted people, when confronted by threats, will be to overreact to them and even to support demagogues who promise to defend our self-interest. Democratic citizens can be manipulated in times of war by self-interest into supporting collectivist ideologies that undermine freedom. In times of war, it is easy to give up private conscience and identify with the whole. And from the point of view of the collective, it is easy to justify war, torture, and other violations of liberty. Self-interested citizens want comfort, safety, and peace; they will thus willingly submit to repressive and unjust policies, so long as their economic self-interest is maximized. This helps to explain democratic support for actions that violate principles of liberal-democratic justice.

The solution to this problem is not, however, the utopia of the philosopher-king. Plato's philosopher-king has too much power; and history shows us that decentralized power is the best defense of liberty. Rather, we must cultivate private conscience and individual virtue on the part of citizens. Citizens need wisdom, courage, patience, moderation, and skepticism toward power. In short, they need what Kant called enlightenment. Each one of us need to continually remind ourselves that private conscience, autonomy, and self-rule have a value independent of the abstract needs of the collective. Self-reliant individuals need to assert the importance of private conscience against the collectivizing tendencies we see in war. The Kantian dream relies upon more and better education about the temptations of collectivism and continued defense of the importance of private conscience. Citizens must understand the tragic flaw that haunts democracy—the flaw indicated by Plato's prophecy: that individuals are often too willing to sacrifice themselves for the Leviathan. By understanding this, citizens can work to develop personal virtues that will allow them to resist the temptations of the demagogues. And by understanding that Kant's dream includes the deontological idea that principles of justice apply even in war, they will be able to resist the temptation to become unjust when they must fight in defense of democracy.

CHAPTER FOUR

DEMOCRATIC CONTROL AND PROFESSIONAL ETHICS

If there is one basic element in our Constitution, it is civilian control of the military.

> *Harry S. Truman (Dallek, 2008, 119)*

Plato worried that security cannot be left to just anyone. We need a skilled and virtuous group of professionals to act as guardians for society. However, history reminds us that these guardians themselves must be supervised by the citizens whose interests they serve. The idea of civilian control of the military is essential to modern democratic politics.

One of the most important examples of the assertion of civilian control was President Truman's firing of General MacArthur during the Korean War. MacArthur had wanted to expand the war into China and to use nuclear weapons against North Korea in order to create a radiation belt that would prevent the Chinese from invading, and he openly challenged the President's foreign policy. Truman asserted his Presidential authority and removed MacArthur. Perhaps by asserting civilian control, Truman averted a broader and more violent war. More recent events remind us that at times, however, we might want the military to resist civilian control in order to avoid moral and strategic blunders. Perhaps the war in Iraq could have been avoided or fought differently if the military had more power to resist the decisions of President Bush and his Secretary of Defense, Donald Rumsfeld. These two episodes should remind us that there are no easy answers here. Overly zealous military leaders can lead the nation into dangerous strategic blunders; but the same is true of overly zealous civilian leaders. The principle of civilian control and the feedback loop set up by public debate is the best solution we've got. But there is no final solution here. Instead, the issue of civilian control is another example of the difficulty of moral judgment in war.

DEMOCRACY AND CIVILIAN CONTROL

In liberal democracies, civilian authorities and the constitutional system establish the ends for which the guardians work; but the guardians choose the proper means to obtain these ends, based upon professional expertise and the code of ethics governing their profession. This leads inevitably to conflict: between the people's right to democratic control of the military and the soldier's right to professional role autonomy, between the public's interest and the soldier's "private" professional judgment.

It might seem out of place to use the term "private" to describe the sphere of professional judgment of public servants such as soldiers—but professional judgments are private insofar as they are limited in scope and in accord with the standards of a particular profession (see Hansson, 2007). In other words, the soldier's professional expertise is limited to the role and profession he occupies. And this role and profession is—in a democracy—supposed to be governed by the people. The difficulty is that although the people usually lack the expertise to properly govern the military, constitutional republican systems of government expect professional soldiers to obey the will of the people.

In a democracy, despite inevitable differences in expertise that occur because of the division of labor, each citizen is entitled to make judgments about the justice of war. Indeed, perhaps more so than in other fields of ethical concern, judgments about war must be opened to broad democratic debate. This is true because in a democracy the consent of the governed is the key to legitimacy. Direct and explicit consent is not required on a daily basis since most of the mundane issues of governance are less important than war. But war is one of the most momentous concerns of a nation. War affects the whole nation in profound ways: wars require vast expenditures; they have long-term international and political consequences; and they have a deep impact on the lives of soldiers and their families. But most significantly, war is a moral problem.

When wars are fought, soldiers are asked to kill in the name of the nation and they are asked to put themselves at risk of being killed. War is thus not a routine matter of government. In routine matters, decision making can be delegated to representatives and bureaucrats. However, war is of such importance to the moral, economic, and political health of the nation, that a very strong case can be made that it requires direct and ongoing consent for its democratic justification. Unfortunately, direct and ongoing consent is difficult to enact and institutionalize because war is by its very nature undemocratic. Moreover, ordinary citizens lack the virtues, expertise, and experience to make good judgments about war.

The war in Iraq may seem to show us a failure of deliberative democracy, especially for those who opposed the war (see Gutmann and Thompson, 2004). Critics of the war have claimed that the fact that the war broke out despite protests to the contrary shows us a failure of democracy both within the United States and in the global system in which the United States acts as hegemon. Such a claim obviously begs the question about whether the war was in fact justified and prejudges the outcome of deliberative democratic debate. One could argue, in fact, that the deliberative process used in the run-up to the war reached the legitimate conclusion that the war was morally permissible. After all, despite widespread protest, the majority of the American people were in favor of the war and the U.S. Congress supported the war effort. But if the war was unjust, the fact that the majority approved it shows us that the people are not good judges of the morality of war.

A further problem arose in the war on terrorism, in light of the fact that the civilian authorities proposed methods that appeared to run counter to the values of the military and its own code of ethics, that is, in the debate about the use of interrogative torture. A notable expression of this can be seen in a letter (dated September 12, 2006) to the Senate's Armed Forces Committee that was signed by 38 retired officers including 2 former Chairmen of the Joint Chiefs of Staff.[1] These officers argued that the United States should abide by Common Article 3 of the Geneva Conventions, which require humane and fair treatment of prisoners. In opposition to the civilian authorities in the Bush Administration, the retired officers argued that the military has long abided by this standard and that the standard serves the interests of American military personnel.

Here is the problem. On the one hand, in liberal democracies we want the military to be under the control of the civilian authorities. But there are times when the civilian authorities will go too far—as Plato predicted. Thus, we also want some degree of professional role autonomy for the military. The danger, however, is that an independent military force poses a risk for democracy itself.

The basic notion of democratic deliberation is that social decisions should be made by free and open debate among equal citizens. One key concept of deliberative democracy is the ideal of fair procedural justice, as articulated by John Rawls. The key to a just constitutional system is the fairness of its procedures for making decisions of public interest and the basic idea of social cooperation based upon reciprocity and mutual advantage. A long tradition extending from Kant to Rawls claims that wars fought in the name of democracy should be limited by principles of justice such as we find in the just war tradition. Rawls assumes that well-ordered peoples will agree with these principles, while Kant describes these as necessary conditions for the beginning of peace among nations—what he calls "preliminary articles of peace," which include prohibitions against aggression, the use of poisons and assassins, and a call for the abolition of standing armies.

Liberals like Kant and Rawls hope that public deliberation about war would lead to a moral framework quite similar to the just war theory. Moreover, Kant and Rawls argue that democracy is itself the source of lasting peace. In democracy, as Rawls imagines it, there is peace by satisfaction: human needs are satisfied and "liberal peoples have nothing to go to war about" (Rawls, 1999b, 47). The hope, then, is that procedures and institutions of liberal democracy will not only serve to ground war on public reasons, but they will also serve to defuse the drive to war and keep warfare within moral limits. Unfortunately, Plato's worry has returned. We've seen in recent years that democratic peoples can support wars with causes that are not clearly just, such as the invasion of Iraq, while also supporting methods that violate principles of *jus in bello*—such as the use of torture.

Wars that are fought by democracies in the name of democratic values should be based upon decisions that have broad democratic legitimacy. For those who defend the liberal idea of deliberative democracy, legitimate decisions of government are understood as resulting from reasonable procedures of public deliberation. Now clearly, it is impossible for every issue of national concern to be subject to extensive public deliberation and a national referendum: human rights cannot be violated even by the vote of a majority. Indeed, some decisions—such as national security matters—must be decided upon quickly and they require a sort of expertise and specialization that the public does not possess. Nor is deliberative democracy merely a version of majority rules in which everything must be subjected to a referendum. Nonetheless, the ideal is one in which there is supposed to be as much openness and reasonable public debate among equal citizens as possible (where public reasons are those that aim at creating consensus amid diversity by appealing to shared constitutional principles). If we apply this idea to the justification of war, the idea of public deliberation results in the following ideal that would be shared by thinkers such as Kant and Rawls: legitimate decisions about war should be the result of (1) free public deliberation that is as open and extensive as possible in light of limitations imposed on such deliberation by the nature of the topic; and (2) such decisions should be grounded in publicly shared principles that allow for consensus that is grounded in constitutional principles, such as basic principles of human rights, which would limit war.

The second clause would prevent wars from being fought for sectarian purposes. Decisions about war cannot then be based upon claims about the self-interest of a certain industry or group; they cannot be based upon claims about personality or individual preference; and they cannot be based upon religious claims. The purpose of the second clause is to ensure that wars are fought for democratic purposes that are consensus values for the diverse members of the democratic polity. Among these consensus values, we would presume to find basic human rights. Democratic states should thus avoid wars and strategies that violate human rights.

Unfortunately, just as the Korean war of the Truman era involved atrocities—in the use of Napalm against North Korea and the scorched earth approach to the war—the war on terrorism has also pushed the envelope in terms of human rights, although the human rights violations of the present war have been mitigated by a military ethic that is less sanguine about collateral damage than Truman era commanders like MacArthur. Indeed, the new situation of the war on terrorism is that military professionals have been the source of resistance to the civilian authorities' push for violations of just war principles and human rights. This might lead us to conclude that professional military judgment should trump the results of open democratic deliberation. But the fact remains that there is no final solution to this problem. Instead, there is an uneasy dialectic between military experts and civilian authorities. Again, the best solution we've stumbled upon is extensive and open public deliberation.

Nonetheless, there are at least three limitations to the process of open and extensive public deliberation:

1. Limitations that are imposed by demands for immediate responses to urgent threats.
2. Limitations that are imposed by the need for secrecy with regard to issues concerning national security.
3. Limitations that are imposed by the division of labor in society, especially the need for specialized knowledge and professional expertise among national security professionals.

These limitations create a problem for establishing an entirely open and equal procedure for democratic deliberation about war. The question is to what degree we should either embrace these limitations or seek to overcome them. There is a continuum here that can be analyzed in terms of conservative or Platonic vs. liberal or Kantian points of view.

Some may argue that the public interest is furthered by allowing for a large area of secret and autonomous decision-making in war that is governed by the professional code of the military itself. This conservative or Platonic point of view holds that the guardians of society must act autonomously for the good of the society they protect. Thus, for the conservative, the limitations mentioned above carve out a niche of autonomous action for military professionals and their civilian superiors who work on national defense. Conservatives hold that there are significant and immediate threats to be controlled through the use of military power; and that these threats are best met by a disciplined military force that is free to act without the hindrance of extended public deliberation. The conservative view will also maintain that the military's professional judgment about legitimate means should not be subordinated to the nonexpert judgment of the civilian authority.

One could justify the conservative idea by claiming that a large degree of military autonomy can be democratically legitimated, as long as it is the result of a fair procedure and prior public deliberation in Rawls' sense. In other words, the public might decide that its guardians should have a significant degree of autonomy and create procedures that delegate the power for decision making about war to the guardians. These guardians are supervised by civilian authorities who are themselves representatives of the people. Democratic deliberation occurs at the level of thinking about the procedures for establishing and supporting military power and also through the indirect process of electing civilian authorities who have control over military power and military spending. From the conservative perspective, democratic deliberation should have very little impact on decisions about whether a given war should be fought or how it should be fought. These decisions should be left to the experts.

The conservative approach is not implausible. Indeed, one might argue that the conservative approach is typical of the system of military power in the United States. And one might argue that the conservative ideal—if it had been more robustly applied—would have reduced the moral outrages of the war on terrorism.

The more liberal view holds that professional autonomy for the military is dangerous. While some professional autonomy is inevitable given the limitations outlined above, the people have an interest in reducing military autonomy as much as possible to insure that the costs of war (moral, political, and economic) do not become unbearable. For the liberal approach, the question of who guards the guardians is an important concern, with the answer being that the civilian authority should be in charge.

Liberals tend to worry that the guardians' military spirit must be restrained in the name of peace and justice. Kant and other thinkers of the Enlightenment held that the key to peace would be for democratic peoples to restrain military power by controlling the military's purse strings. If the people were asked if they wanted to pay for war, Kant claims, they would be unlikely to consent. And so there would be fewer wars. For the liberal, the effect of any limitation on public deliberation that is necessitated by the division of labor should be minimized and the public should be empowered to participate in decisions about war. However, if we accept civilian control and the liberal ideal, it is possible to end up with the problem foreseen by Plato: that civilian authorities will use military

power in immoral or imprudent ways and the people will be persuaded by the demagogues to support wars and tactics that military professionals reject as immoral or ill-advised.

PROFESSIONAL ETHICS AND THE SEPARATIST THESIS

Despite his conflict with Truman, MacArthur remained committed
to basic principles of military ethics. In his farewell speech at West
Point in 1962, he eulogized the military profession, whose code of
"Duty, Honor, Country" embodies the "highest moral laws and will
stand the test of any ethics or philosophies ever promulgated for
the uplift of mankind." He went on to say that civilian politicians
can wrangle about politics—but that soldiers are supposed to be
concerned only with the issue that defines the purpose of military
service: national defense.

MacArthur indicates that the military has an ethos of its own
that is to some extent divorced from the ethics of ordinary life. The
Platonic point of view emphasizes that the warrior class has its own
unique code of ethics. Plato suggested that the guardians would
have to live communally. They would not possess money. And their
behaviors—including their sexuality—would be strictly controlled.
Liberals tend to think of questions of justice as if they should be
of universal concern: everyone should be concerned with the question of justice in war and all members of society should be treated
equally. The current discussion of homosexuality and marital fidelity in the American military is a case in point. On the one hand, the
military needs to control its soldiers' libidos to prevent abuse and
create unity and good morale. But modern liberal democracies tend
to be more permissive with regard to sexual ethics, encouraging a
laissez-faire attitude. On the issue of sexuality, as on other issues,
there is a clash between the point of view of the military profession
and the values of liberal democracy.

The ethics of war itself can appear to be only of concern for soldiers. It is possible to understand just war theory simply as a matter of professional ethics that is not the concern of the rest of us.
We often divide ethical standards up in this way in accord with the
division of labor in society. Codes of professional ethics are oriented toward those professionals who engage in activities defined
by the profession. While all individuals might have an interest in
ensuring that professionals behave well, the agents whose specific

responsibilities are defined by these codes constitute a limited sub-set of society: doctors are the agents governed by codes of medical ethics; business people are ruled by codes of business ethics; and soldiers are subject to the rules of the just war theory. Platonists will see this as normal and inevitable. Plato routinely appeals to the specialized expertise of those who actually know what they are talking about. Liberals tend to reject or seek to limit inequalities stemming from a differentiated system because such a system can create an unequal and hierarchical social structure. Moreover, we all have an interest in the behavior of doctors, businesspersons, and soldiers because their behavior affects us either directly or indirectly. Thus, we should each have a voice in establishing and enforcing professional codes of ethics, while at the same time, the professionals know best when it comes to their code of ethics.

The liberal thesis is that in a democracy all citizens have a respons-ibility to judge the justness of wars that are fought in their names. The problem is that not all citizens have the requisite expertise to make good judgments about the justness of any given war. Indeed, we've seen that civilian authorities have made faulty judgments in the war on terrorism and that the people have supported these mistaken judgments. Nonetheless, if we do not want to return to Plato's centralized authoritarian ideal, the only solution is broader and better democratic control. First, the military and the govern-ment should be as open and honest as possible, so that citizens can adequately scrutinize the facts about any given war. Second, cit-izens have a duty to educate themselves about these facts and about foreign affairs in general. And third, all parties—the military, the government, and the citizenry—need to educate themselves about the just war theory so that they can make good moral judgments about the facts at hand.

This is an ideal that assumes honesty and moral compunction on the part of all members of society. I recognize that there are limita-tions to this in practice; however, we must be clear about the ideal, lest we succumb to the temptation to reject democratic control out of hand, when in fact we have not yet given it a chance.

The liberal-democratic approach appears to run counter to the so-called 'separatist thesis' in professional ethics (see Gewirth, 1986 and Freedman, 1978). The separatist thesis holds that professionals have rights and duties unique to themselves. But it is important to remember that every profession is defined by the larger social and moral context. The means employed by the professional who executes his institutionally defined duty are justified by the institutionally defined roles of the profession. It is obvious that there must be some degree of professional role autonomy. But professional activities are also subject to general moral principles which impose social and personal limits on professional autonomy.

It is not surprising that professional practitioners resent those amateurs who judge without knowledge. This resentment is perhaps most severe with regard to the question of war. Soldiers make profound sacrifices, sacrifices whose value is called into question both by those who deny the legitimacy of a just war and by those who encourage soldiers to fight unjustly in unjust wars. It is not surprising that soldiers might argue that non-soldiers, who lack expertise about the sorts of sacrifices they make—physical, emotional, and moral—should leave the military alone to make these judgments in "private," as it were. This resentment can be further fostered by the fact that soldiers and civilian leaders have access to classified information that, quite simply, cannot be shared with the rest of society. However, the liberal Kantian view is grounded in the Enlightenment belief that most humans are in fact capable of moral judgment. One does not need to be a murderer to know that murder is wrong. But we do need to know the relevant facts about murder and about morality in order to make the judgment. Likewise, citizens need to understand the just war theory and the historical and political issues involved in particular wars in order to make good judgments. Again, liberals believe that we are intelligent enough to do this—we merely need better education and better access to relevant information. But conservatives will claim that we should leave the guardians alone to do their duty.

CONCLUSION

This is a serious conflict between rival goods: the good of democratic control and the good of professional autonomy for military experts. The danger of professional specialization and the separatist thesis is that it can stifle public debate and undermine democratic control. A thorough application of the separatist thesis in the case of war would take judgments about war out of the hands of the people in whose interests the warriors are supposed to fight, leaving it up to them to decide what is in the national interest—as

MacArthur apparently did during the Korean conflict. The separatist thesis tends to lead to a fragmentation of ethical concern and responsibility. It also tends to foster what Weber called "bureaucratic rationality": the inability or unwillingness of the professional to judge his activity from a more general perspective. And this in turn can lead to the bureaucratized sort of "banal" evil that Arendt analyzed in her discussion of Adolph Eichmann—where efficiency becomes divorced from moral reflection.

A thoroughgoing separatism in professional ethics misunderstands the nature of the division of labor. We divide labor in order to maximize efficiency in society as a whole, not in order to fragment society into sequestered, mutually suspicious fields. Society as a whole ought to govern each of the specializations created within the division of labor because the division of labor is itself created in order to secure the interests of the whole. This is especially true with regard to war. It is the whole of society that suffers the consequences of warfare, thus society as a whole ought to be in charge of regulating it.

Professionals, even professional soldiers, remain human persons who ought to be concerned with basic moral principles. Soldiers are human beings who ought to be concerned about justice and about the attitudes and ideas of the non-soldiers with whom they must work and to whom they are related through a variety of social ties. Professionals in any field cannot forget that roles defined by their professional institutions are themselves supported by society as a whole and subject to moral limits.

Democratic equality and openness do not require that the division of labor be effaced. However, democracies do generally require that specialized professions justify themselves in easily comprehensible terms to the rest of society (see Bertram, 1997). It also requires as much of an end to secrecy as is feasible while preserving security. Finally, democracy requires that citizens educate themselves and make informed judgments. These requirements tend to reinforce one another. When the government does not trust the people to make informed judgments it tends to move toward secrecy, lies, and propaganda; and the people are left without relevant information. The solution to this is for the government to become more open and for the people to educate themselves. Expertise and specialization are not necessarily antithetical to democracy. However, as Arthur Applbaum has concluded, dissenters are "foolish and morally irresponsible" if they do not seek out the facts possessed by experts (Applbaum, 1992, 273). This implies that democratic citizens should make use of the expertise of military personnel and civilian leadership when judging whether a war is just. It also demands that our leaders should be willing to engage citizens in serious moral dialogue and not succumb to the temptations of demagoguery.

The responsibility of a citizen in a self-governing democracy is to question and demand proof, especially when considering the momentous moral, political, and historical implications of war. Moreover, the responsibility of a democratic military is to be as open as possible about the causes and means of war. The military, the citizenry, and the civilian authority should not be in mutually hostile relationship in which they do not trust one another. Nonetheless, a certain dialectical antagonism is helpful. It helped to prevent MacArthur from launching a nuclear war in the Korean peninsula. And more antagonism would have helped to prevent mistaken judgment in the war on terrorism.

NOTE

1.   The letter can be found on Human Rights First website: www.human-rightsfirst.info/pdf/06913-etn-military-let-ca3.pdf

CHAPTER FIVE

THE MILITARY ESTABLISHMENT

*Overgrown military establishments are under any form of govern-
ment inauspicious to liberty, and are to be regarded as particularly
hostile to republican liberty.*
                        George Washington, "Farewell Address"

War can be a means of spreading democracy and establishing cohesion in a diverse society. Progress toward democracy has occurred
by way of military adventures in the United States. Civil rights have
been extended in various ways that can be correlated with the great
wars of American history. The Revolutionary War helped extend
rights to white males. The Civil War helped to extend rights to
former slaves. And the two World Wars of the twentieth century can
be correlated with increased rights for minorities and for women.
When masses of men (and women) bear arms in defense of the state,
the values of the state have to come to reflect the values of those
who fight for it. Consider the case of the Japanese-Americans who
served in the Second World War, when their families were unjustly
imprisoned in concentration camps at home. Or consider the way
that protests against the Vietnam War were correlated with civil
rights protests in the 1960s. Military service provides a path to
citizenship and equality, while wars unite people en masse in ways
that can have a progressive impact on domestic politics. Admittedly,
warfare and militarism are not ideal paths toward democracy. But
history is not ideal.

Max Weber explained the link between democracy and militarism
as follows: "the basis of democratization is everywhere purely
military in character" (Weber, 1950, 325). Bruce Porter claims that
suffrage rights were extended throughout the past several centuries

according to the basic idea, "one gun, one vote" (Porter, 1994, xvii). As diverse people serve the state, the state recognizes this service with expanded citizenship rights. We can see this sort of process today in the way that foreign nationals are offered a path to citizenship as a reward for military service. When military service is widely extended, so too are the burdens, responsibilities, and rights of citizenship.

While war can have this progressive impact in the domestic arena, it can also have the reverse affect. Critics of war and defenders of liberty have long noted that war tends to produce centralization of power that comes at the expense of individual liberty. One obvious mechanism by which this happens is via conscription. Conscription uses individuals in ways that are opposed to the basic liberal-democratic ideal of individual human rights. Armies are not organized in a democratic fashion. And decisions about going to war are often based upon secret information and the judgment of experts: it is rare that "the people" are asked to vote on going to war. Moreover, civil rights are routinely curtailed during wartime: during the Second World War, Japanese-Americans were imprisoned in concentration camps; and civil rights have been threatened during the war on terrorism by provisions in the Patriot Act and by the use of torture, indefinite detention and denial of habeas corpus rights. Civil rights violations are a symptom of the larger philosophical problem: during wartime, utilitarian calculations take precedence over deontological prohibitions that protect individuality and limit state action. The result can be a military establishment that is, in George Washington's words, "inauspicious to liberty.

The paradox to be discussed in this chapter is thus that warfare is both a peril and a promise for democratic politics. The perils include the creation of a professional warrior class at odds with civilian authorities, the burden of war taxes, and violations of civil liberties. But war also provides a democratizing mechanism that can help to build a sense of citizenship and a broad sense of public-spirited service.

THE ENLIGHTENMENT IDEAL AND THE U.S. CONSTITUTION

The problem of military autonomy and the growth of military establishments was a serious concern for the American founders and for political philosophers during the Enlightenment. Kant's plan for perpetual peace, for example, called for the end of stand-ing armies. And Kant thought that the way to limit war would be to ask for consent from the people whose taxes were used to support war and the military establishment. The fact that wars and military establishments require taxation and debt was a significant problem for the American founders. In 1795, the same year that Kant pub-lished his essay, *Perpetual Peace*, James Madison noted that war tends to create oligarchic centralized power:

> Of all enemies to public liberty, war is perhaps the most to be dreaded, because it comprises and develops the germ of every other. War is the parent of armies; from these proceed debts and taxes; and armies, and debts, and taxes are the known instruments for bringing the many under the domination of the few. In war, too, the discretionary power of the Executive is extended . . . and all the means of seducing the minds, are added to those of subdu-ing the force, of the people. (Madison, 1795/1865, 491–492)

Madison concluded, "no nation could preserve its freedom in the midst of continual warfare." A few decades later Tocqueville agreed: "There is no long war that does not put freedom at great risk in a democratic country" (Tocqueville, 2002, 621). War produces a need for centralization and increases in the prerogatives of central government. Not only is power concentrated in the Executive dur-ing war but, as Madison notes, the Executive may feel obliged to "seduce the minds of the people" in order to create support for the war effort.

Tocqueville and Madison both note that when war-fighting (and subsequent rebuilding efforts) extend for years and decades, taxation and centralization are inevitable. A similar problem occurs even in peacetime, when standing armies are maintained at public expense in preparation for war. In *Federalist* no. 41, Madison reminds us that Roman liberty was destroyed by her military power. And he goes on to show us the dilemma: in a world of armed nations, we need an army at the ready; but a ready force tends to undermine liberty. Standing armies that become too autonomous pose a serious threat for democracy. Alexander Hamilton recognized this problem in *Federalist* nos. 28 and 29. George Washington noted the problem in his "Farewell Address." And in 1961, another General who became President, Dwight

Eisenhower, warned in his own Farewell Address against the growth of the "military-industrial complex."

The presumption of the American Founders and other defenders of democracy such as Tocqueville and Kant was that democratic governments should not have standing armies and that they should avoid extended wars. Moreover, these Enlightenment thinkers assumed that democratic peoples would not consent to support standing armies and expansive wars. At the same time, as Madison noted in *Federalist* no. 41, a standing army may be necessary, especially in a world in which war is the rule, rather than the exception. Moreover, military service is a good way of instilling patriotism and national pride. The problem is that those who serve are more likely to believe that war is a good thing. Military personnel who view the military as a career will see war as providing the best way to advance. Tocqueville noted that in a democracy, equal opportunity in the military provides a way to advance economically and socially. War accelerates these opportunities.

But this is why liberals such as Kant argue that democratic governance and civilian control of the military are needed: to reign in military personnel who are more willing to go to war than other people who have to pay for it with their tax money. The idea of civilian control is central to democratic politics. Richard Kohn puts this idea as follows: "While a country may have civilian control of the military without democracy, it cannot have democracy without civilian control" (Kohn, 1997, 141). Without civilian control, democracies risk being transformed into military dictatorships. It is the tradition of civilian control and the military's allegiance to the principles of democracy that prevent this from happening.

Civilian control does not need to be tied to democracy. Clausewitz, for example, recognized that political leaders should control the military. Clausewitz claims that war is "the continuation of politics by other means." So the military must be subordinated to the political leadership. If war is about politics, then war should be under the control of the political authorities who provide the "intelligent faculty" of the state, as Clausewitz puts it (Clausewitz, 1982, 405). Clausewitz' idea appears to fit better with a Platonic ideal in which the political authorities are indeed, the intelligent faculty.

In a democracy, rather than emphasizing control by the intelligent faculty, civilian control means that warriors should be subordinated to the will of the people. There is the risk of mob rule here—as Plato noted. But those modern democracies that developed out of the Enlightenment are not ruled by the mob, as Plato feared. Rather, the Kantian "republican" model includes a written constitution, explicit recognition of human rights, and a system of representation. In modern democracy, the military's responsibility to the people is usually indirect, since democratic control of the military is exercised in two ways: through the Constitution itself and through the peoples' representatives. The oath of the U.S. Army requires soldiers to swear to "support and defend the Constitution" as well as to promise to obey the orders of the President. This double oath requires allegiance to the democratic institutions of the American system as well as loyalty to the current representative of the will of the people who is acting as commander-in-chief.

In the United States, the principle of civilian control is found in the Constitution itself. Article 2, Section 2 of the Constitution gives the President the power to control the military as commander-in-chief. Article 1, Section 8 gives Congress the right to pay for the military and the power to declare war. The Constitution thus mandates civilian control of the military via the people's representatives. And in pledging an oath to the Constitution, American soldiers thus affirm the idea of civilian control.

CHALLENGES FOR CIVILIAN CONTROL

Civilian control in democracies is not without its problems. About 50 years ago, Samuel Huntington indicated that members of the military profession tend to be more conservative than the general population. "The military view of man is thus decidedly pessimistic . . . The man of the military ethic is essentially the man of Hobbes" (Huntington, 1957, 63). This point has become more obvious as the volunteer army in the United States has become more Republican and more Christian than the mainstream. Martin Cook describes the American military as "unrepresentative" of the people and "deeply alienated" from society (Cook, 2004, ix). For Cook, the obvious point is that the military is "overwhelmingly Republican in its politics." More recently, Jeffrey Sharlet has chronicled the growth of fundamentalist evangelical Christianity among the ranks of the officer corps in the American military (Sharlet, 2009). Moreover, military service tends to run in families, with military families living quite differently than the mainstream.

Huntington further argues that liberals are generally suspicious of military virtues such as obedience. According to Huntington, liberals tend to think that "national defense is the responsibility of all, not just a few. If war becomes necessary, the state must fight as a nation in arms relying on popular militias and citizen armies" (Huntington, 1957, 91). One of the reasons that liberals may be skeptical of the professional military is because the volunteer army is not broadly representative of the people. When there is a genuine citizen-army that fights for a truly national cause, the assumption is that there will be extensive democratic deliberation about such a war; this is also true when the costs of war are widely and equally shared. But an autonomous professional fighting force may not be concerned with the democratic process. Moreover, when there is a ruling elite who makes decisions about how to employ this fighting force, the worry is that the nation will be involved in more wars and more unjustified wars.

The idea of civilian control holds that political leaders who are civilians and who are responsive to the people should have power over the military hierarchy. This idea can be grounded in the just war idea of "legitimate authority." Those who advocate civilian control claim that in democracy only duly elected civilian leaders possess legitimate authority. There are two ways that civilian control can be further analyzed, corresponding to the difference between *jus ad bellum* and *jus in bello* in just war theory. What we might call *"ad bellum* civilian control" means that civilian leaders are responsible for making decision about *which* wars the military fights. In addition, *"in bello* civilian control" is the idea that civilian leaders are responsible for decisions about *how* wars are fought. The usual way of coordinating these two ideas is to hold that civilian leaders should have the final say in *ad bellum* decisions, while military leaders should be allowed greater autonomy to decide the *in bello* question. This fits with the usual way of analyzing the just war theory. The question of going to war is a political question that must be answered by legitimate political authorities. But questions about *jus in bello* are part of what Walzer calls "the war convention," which is primarily a professional concern for soldiers. Indeed, Walzer goes so far as to claim that *in bello* and *ad bellum* principles are "logically independent"

(Walzer, 1977, 21). According to this idea, it is possible for a soldier to fight unjustly in pursuit of a just cause; and it is possible for a soldier to fight justly in pursuit of an unjust cause. Given this logical independence, conservatives might argue that civilian authorities should have less to say about the *in bello* question of how war is fought and instead leave this up to the professionals. But liberals will claim that the civilian authority should also judge *how* war is fought. There are good reasons for the civilian authority to delegate responsibility for *in bello* judgments to the military authorities who are more competent to make such judgments. But since war concerns us all, liberals will argue for more extensive civilian control.

Civilian control of the military is a fragile product of the human spirit. It is based upon ideas and virtues and not upon force. Plato raised the question of who will guard the guardians in the *Republic*. There is always a risk that the guardians may turn against the people. Plato's solution was to train the guardians in a life of virtue. Their sense of justice, duty, and loyalty would prevent them from turning against the people. Democratic control of the military extends this idea by claiming that the people are wise enough to guard the guardians. This ideal is based upon the sort of respect for persons and for the rule of law that is cultivated in a democracy and that is essential to the notion of democratic citizenship.

Soldiers are to be democratic citizens as well, where citizenship implies a commitment to the ideals of democracy. One of the reasons that liberals might advocate the idea of the citizen-army that is broadly and equally representative of society as a whole is to ensure that military personnel themselves represent and adhere to the principles for which they are asked to fight. The danger of an entirely professional army of paid volunteers or mercenaries is that there is no guarantee that these guardians are committed to the values that they are supposed to be guarding. For democratic control to be successful, then, soldiers have to be citizens who are committed to the ideals of democratic citizenship. In a democracy, it seems that the soldier should identify himself primarily as a citizen of the nation who is subject to the requirements of democratic citizenship.

It may thus be troubling that the American volunteer army is made up of many noncitizens—roughly 30,000 soldiers. Some claim that it is a virtue of the American military that it is open to noncitizens and that serving in the military as a "green-card warrior" provides a path to citizenship. Others argue that we are hiring a mercenary army while also making it easier for the rest of our citizens to avoid the obligation (and the education) of military service.

In thinking about civilian control of the military it is easy to romanticize the idea of a democratic army made up of "citizen-soldiers." The romantic ideal of the citizen-soldiers of a democratic army includes the following. These soldiers are supposed to be ideologically committed to the cause for which they fight; and this cause is linked to democratic values and democratic patriotism. These soldiers are supposed to be representative of the nation for whom they fight in terms of class, race, religion, regional affiliation, and other sorts of characteristics. They are supposed to be fundamentally civilian: they fight temporarily but have other nonmilitary career aspirations. These soldiers are supposed to be citizens, with the full set of rights of any other citizen of the democracy. And finally, these citizen-soldiers are supposed to have faith in the institutions of civil society, the institutions of democratic governance, and the basic idea of civilian control of the military. This ideal is connected with the idea that warfare and military service are beneficial to the spread of democratic values at home.

However, this ideal does not obtain in reality. Not only does the American military include some noncitizens but often the military is not just a temporary job engaged in for a good cause: rather it is a career path. Moreover, some of those who fight our wars are not regular military but CIA agents and mercenary forces who do not fit the romantic profile of the citizen-soldier. In Iraq, for example, the United States has employed quite a few "privatized military firms": somewhere around 20,000 nonmilitary support personnel (see Singer, 2004). While some of the personnel employed in this way provide logistical support for the regular U.S. military, there are also other mercenary forces who are engaged in providing security in Iraq. One wonders then whether we actually have a true citizen-army. Without a citizen-army, we lose in two ways. On the one hand, citizens are no longer broadly educated about the military and about the ideal of justice in war and the virtues of military service. On the other hand, a military that is made up of noncitizens and citizens with very narrow ideological and political sympathies is dangerous since the warriors may not properly value the broad traditions of democracy and citizen control of the military.

THE CHALLENGE OF CITIZENSHIP

A serious problem for the idea of civilian control in a democracy has to do with whether citizens make decisions based on public goods or based upon private interest. Ignatieff has described the ideal citizen as follows: "through participation the citizen transcends the limits of his private interest and becomes, in his deliberation with others, what Aristotle said man truly was—a political animal" (Ignatieff, 1995, 52). Walzer links this ideal to an account of human flourishing: "to live well is to be politically active, working with our fellow citizens, collectively determining our common destiny—not for the sake of this or that determination but for the work itself, in which our highest capacities as rational and moral agents find expression" (Walzer, 1995, 155). Human beings flourish when they engage in public deliberation as citizens. Citizens ought to be committed to the idea that public deliberation is good and they ought to want to defend the constitutional republic that makes this ideal of citizenship possible.

Liberal defenders of the just war idea—such as Ignatieff and Walzer—maintain that there is a close connection between democratic control and adhering to justice in war. In his recent book, *Arguing About War*, Walzer writes: "as the old saying goes, war is too important to be left to the generals; just war even more so. The ongoing critique of warmaking is a centrally important democratic activity" (Walzer, 2004, 15). Ignatieff explains the notion of democratic critique in much more detail in *The Lesser Evil*. For Ignatieff, the key is the adversarial system that we find institutionalized in the procedures of liberal democracy. These institutions allow for radical disagreement about the substantive outcome of the procedure and so, "no government's answer has the power to lead us either straight to anarchy or to tyranny" (Ignatieff, 2004, 3). Ignatieff notes that recent events in the war on terrorism may undermine our faith that this sort of adversarial system is working properly. The failure with regard to Iraq might lead us to argue that the problem is that civilian leaders have too much power over the military. After all, it was the civilian leadership who made the argument for war, who manipulated intelligence, and who ultimately made the decision to go to war and then to use torture as a means. And many military leaders were opposed to this but unable to speak out against it because of the tradition of civilian control, which led them to defer to the civilian leadership.

One might reasonably argue that we would avoid unjust wars if we allowed the military greater autonomy. This argument has been considered as significant at least since the publication of H.R. McMaster's *Dereliction of Duty*, which chronicled the missteps and lies that led to the Vietnam War. It has returned in discussions of the so-called revolt of the Generals in response to the Bush Administration's mishandling of the war in Iraq. From this point of view, perhaps we should leave war to the generals. It is the military that must do the fighting and make the sacrifices required in war. And moreover, military personnel have a good reason to be concerned with the justice of war: since they do the fighting, their consciences are more profoundly affected by the question of whether they have done the right thing.

One important objection to the idea of democratic control is the fact that the division of labor between the military and civilian spheres entails specialization of expertise and limited access to relevant information. Since secrecy is important for effective military action and since strategic decisions are only understood in light of the complex and often technical details of particular conditions, civilians will always make less informed and less competent judgments about the needs of the military and the requirements of war.

Thus, there is an inevitable conflict between the interests of democracy and the need for secrecy and a military division of labor. On the one hand, every citizen should be concerned with the moral, political, and economic implications of war. But on the other hand, most citizens lack the expertise to make sound judgments about these implications. There is a structural problem here: citizens should demand democratic control of the military; but democratic control will result in inefficient decision-making about our most vital interests.

There are many more problems in the complex relation between civilian authority and the military establishment. Consider, for example, how members of the military establishment often simply ignore or disrespect elected officials: such was the tense relationship between the military and Bill Clinton during the 1990s. Another problem is that civilian leaders, with the cooperation of the military, occasionally engage in actions that are illegal: this happened, for example, in the Iran-Contra scandal of the 1980s. Moreover, consider what happens when civilian leaders refuse the advice of military experts in planning and executing war: this problem occurred as members of the Bush Administration provided insufficient troops to fully deal with the aftermath of the invasion of Iraq.

WARRIOR POLITICS?

Some have argued that we have reached the end of the era of democratic control of the military. In his *Warrior Politics*, Robert Kaplan argues that realpolitik in international affairs requires what he calls a "pagan ethos." What he means by this is that civilian and military leaders must be Machiavellian insofar as they must use power to control unrest and disorder. Kaplan's analysis is linked to a suspicion of democracy that echoes Plato's: democracy produces dangerous disorder and is inefficient in an emergency. Kaplan concludes that, in the twenty-first century, conflicts will require decisive action that cannot be subject to democratic control. He shamelessly states that war must be directed by an elite collaboration between "the Pentagon and corporate America" and that in the future "going to war will be less and less a democratic decision" (Kaplan, 2002, 117).

This is partly a technological problem produced by the reality of terrorism. Modern wars require decisive action in short time frames. In the nineteenth century the idea of deliberative body like the U.S. Congress declaring war made sense, because it took months to amass forces. Today, when forces can be inserted in a matter of hours or days, the military cannot be constrained by the cumbersome process of democratic oversight. In this brave new world, Kaplan says, "the decision to use force will be made autocratically by small groups of civilians and general officers" (Kaplan, 117). Kaplan concludes that the idea of justice in war does not depend on international law or on domestic democratic oversight. Rather, "as in ancient times, this justice will depend upon the moral fiber of military commanders themselves, whose role will often be indistinguishable from those of civilian leaders" (Kaplan, 118).

Kaplan's ideas are frightening for those of us committed to democracy. The Platonic and Machiavellian approach calls for a ruling elite to lead without concern for the uniformed opinions of the masses. The masses should not be trusted to make decisions about justice in war because the masses are not experts about either the specifics of the concrete case or the subtleties of just war theory. In defense of this approach, one must admit that there is undoubtedly something right about the fact that it is ultimately up to our military and civilian leaders to decide whether a given war is just. Our leaders have access to more information than we do and they have more expertise in the details of military science, which would allow them to make judgments about the morality of a proposed action. However, this still leaves the rest of us with the problem of deciding whether to support the judgments made by our leaders: whether to serve when called and whether to pay taxes that support the war effort.

CONCLUSION

People who pay taxes to support military power have a moral right to participate in decisions about how their money is spent. And soldiers (and their families and friends) remain citizens whose voices must be heard. Even when soldiers are not citizens, they remain human beings. Democratic citizens and human beings generally cannot be exempted from the duty of maintaining a good conscience even during their military service. Indeed, a military force that required its citizen-soldiers and its mercenary soldiers to sacrifice their moral integrity during service would be both immoral and a danger to democracy

Military service can, ironically, be a mechanism for spreading democratic values. A citizen-army can be a great melting pot in which diverse citizens learn to work together for the greater good. Indeed, military service has had this affect in the past. Unfortunately, we are moving in the direction of mercenary forces who do not represent the populus. This is a danger for democracy: a professional military force will tend to resent the control of non-professional civilians.

The professional military does excel in military expertise—including moral expertise. From the perspective of military science—and from a perspective that agrees with Plato and other proponents of centralized power—we want the experts in charge. But a standing force of professional soldiers is a danger to democracy, since these professional soldiers will tend to look askance at civilian authorities. Moreover, these professional soldiers will be more willing to invest more of our resources in preparing for war and going to war. The Founders of the American Republic agreed with Kant and others that democracy and peace are endangered by standing armies, military establishments, and the use of mercenary soldiers. But such is the world we live in: an imperfect world in which the conflict between Kantian and Platonic approaches to politics are far from being resolved.

CHAPTER SIX

THE DEMOCRATIC PEACE MYTH: FROM KANT AND MILL TO HIROSHIMA AND BAGHDAD

For men to choose to kill the innocent as a means to their ends is always murder.
        Anscombe, "Mr. Truman's degree" (Anscombe, 1991, 64)

It has been widely held that as democracy spreads, there will be fewer wars and that the wars that are fought will be more just. This idea can be traced back to Kant. It has been developed in recent years by Doyle, Rawls, and others. This idea also inspired the Bush Doctrine and the recent wars in Afghanistan and Iraq. While giving us reason for hope, such ideas should be accepted cautiously. Uncritical acceptance of the ideal of the democratic peace can lead us to fight democratizing wars. There is a mixed lesson to be learned from past democratizing wars and past experience in nation building, even prior to "the war on terrorism" (see Hippel, 2000). When we acknowledge the ambiguous legacy of democratizing wars as well as the difficulty of justifying war in general, we should be more critical of the myth that forcible democratization is a legitimate way to create lasting peace. If we believe the myth that democratizing wars are both morally acceptable and easy to win, we can end up making moral compromises: atrocities can be rationalized as means to forcibly spread democracy in order to build peace.

Evidence of this problem can be found in the example of the Second World War—an example that has been used as the model for the war on terrorism. President Bush routinely invoked the Second World War paradigm in his defenses of the war on terrorism; and he looked to Truman as a model for his own presidency. But Truman supervised the most egregious use of weapons of mass destruction in the history of warfare: the fire bombing of Japan, which culminated in the atomic bomb attacks on Hiroshima and Nagasaki. The Japanese example is often invoked by defenders of the Bush Doctrine as one of the success stories in the history of forced democratization. Japan has become democratic and it remains a close ally of the United States. But what is often overlooked is that the democratization of Japan was the result of a series of atrocities that resulted in the deaths of millions of innocent Japanese.

Idealistic appropriations of the democratic peace theory can be used to rationalize immoral means. Moral and political life is organized around *ideals*. In Kant's sense, ideals are regulative principles with practical power. They are "archetypes" that allow us, in Kant's language, "to measure the degree and the defects of the incomplete" (Kant, 1965a, B597). But Kant reminds us that we must not be deceived about ideals: we can be deluded when we believe that our ideals are easily realizable. It would seem that the democratic peace ideal would be resistant to those manipulations that call for war and that are used to justify atrocity: after all, the democratic peace ideal is about *peace*. But the democratic peace ideal has a sort of mythic power that can seduce us toward wars that fail to live up to the very standards of justice in war that are central to the ideal. The myth of the democratic peace relies upon eschatological hope for a peaceful world. Since war is such a horrible thing, it is easy to believe that the ideal of perpetual peace can be actualized. In order to actualize this hoped-for end of history, earnest idealists are willing to make moral compromises along the way.

This occurs in a quite obvious way when the democratic peace ideal is combined with utilitarianism in a way that was quite clearly foreshadowed by John Stuart Mill. Mill held that English intervention in India and elsewhere was justified because of the benign value of English colonial power. A similar sort of idealism underlies much of American foreign policy. Indeed, straightforward utilitarian calculations were employed in justifying the use of atomic weapons against Japan. As an antidote, I argue that we must remain true to the deontological roots of the democratic peace ideal, as found in Kant, and that we should steadfastly respect deontological prohibitions against the use of indiscriminate and disproportional force. While utilitarian idealism that advocates using unbridled force to spread democracy is understandable, it should be resisted.

Kant does recognize that war can produce progressive change, as we discussed previously. However, it is wrong to deliberately utilize war to promote peace since war is generally an immoral means. This is especially true of modern wars that use weapons of mass destruction—from atomic bombs to high altitude bombardment and the use of cluster bombs and land mines. These indiscriminate weapons are immoral. In *Perpetual Peace*, Kant condemns "a war of extermination in which both parties and right itself might all be simultaneously annihilated" (Kant, 1991d, 96). Although the use of weapons of mass destruction in the Second World War did eventually result in a peace among reconstituted democracies of German and Japan, this peace was obtained at the expense of morality. We should surely hope for a world in which liberal democracies live in peace; but this hope should not mislead us into thinking that war may be used as a means toward actualizing the ideal, especially in the era of weapons of mass destruction.

THE DARK SIDE OF THE ENLIGHTENMENT MYTH

Support for democratizing war fits within the broader context of the Enlightenment, which was interested in defending and disseminating the idea of the universal rights of man. But the dark side of the Enlightenment ideal is the attempt to spread human rights at the point of a gun. If rights are universal and if democracy brings peace, then it may appear to be acceptable to use force to spread these values. This sort of idealism motivated many supporters of the invasion of Iraq in 2003. But naïve idealism prevents us from seeing the dangers of democratizing wars and the ambiguous legacy of Enlightenment idealism. This ambiguity might be summarized in the close connection between Enlightenment idealism and Western colonialism, in the intimate relationship between the enlightened ideals of human rights discourse and the dark side of imperial ambition.

We see the tension between Enlightenment idealism and the dark side of colonialism in the similarities and differences between Kant and Mill. Kant articulated a deontological grounding for the hope of the democratic peace in the basic ideal of respect for persons and the rights of man. But like most Europeans of the eighteenth century, Kant thought that the white race was superior, an idea which he evidently developed from reading Hume and Herder (see Kant, 2004, 113; also see Gorkom, 2008 or Bernasconi, 2001). However, Kant did not advocate colonial expansion in the name of Enlightenment as Mill did. Mill justified the use of force to bring Enlightenment to those who were benighted by what he termed "savagery" and "barbarism." Mill's project fits well within the nineteenth century idea of the "White Man's Burden" to bring light to the dark-skinned peoples of the world. While we can no longer accept the racist ideas we find in Kant and Mill, it is understandable that those who think of themselves as civilized would want to spread civilization—especially if they believe that the spread of civilization is useful both for the barbarians who are being civilized and for the stability and peace of the international order. Although the temptation to succumb to mythic idealism about democracy and civilization is understandable, it remains wrong.

The important difference between utilitarianism and deontology is found in the difference between public policy and private morality. Utilitarianism aims at creating good outcomes for large numbers of people. Deontological ethics wants to ensure respect for persons and for absolute principles of morality. Utilitarianism is willing to make short-term moral compromises in order to produce long-term benefits. Deontological ethics warns against such moral compromises and admonishes us to remain committed to basic moral principles. Moreover, Kantian deontology and the entire perspective of Kant's critical philosophy remind us not to allow idealism to lead us into moral compromises.

Utilitarian appropriations of the democratic peace ideal should be limited by deontological principles, which oppose wars of democratization. Such a deontological prohibition is best understood from a Kantian point of view. Although Mill also indicates some reasons for a limited approach to democratization, utilitarians are liable to be swept up in a fever to improve the world that leads to flirtations with the dark side. This desire to improve has an admirable quality: it is grounded in hope for improvement. But it is better to stay in the light along with Kant and keep our desire for progress within moral limits. This might mean that we have to admit that progress is slower than we'd like. We must continue to hope that democratic ideals will spread because of some basic truths about human nature, that is, that all human beings desire to be free. We should continue to hope that the democratic peace will dawn and that enlightenment will develop. But we should not take forceful action in order to foster that sort of development.

Forceful utilitarian interventions can actually subvert this process because although human beings desire to be free, they resent freedom that is forced upon them. Mill himself recognized this idea, even though he was willing to flirt with the idea of forcing freedom upon people. For Mill, the idea of "nonintervention" only applies in *European* affairs, that is, among the civilized. Mill does not extend nonintervention to the barbarians. Despite his advocacy of liberty, Mill succumbed to the temptation of paternalism: he thought that non-Europeans were incapable of struggling for freedom themselves because of their spiritual immaturity. Such racist and colonialist attitudes are the dark side of the Enlightenment.

Democratic idealism remains a fact in international affairs—as seen in the Bush Doctrine and the wars in Afghanistan and Iraq. The aggressive use of war by the United States to defend and disseminate democracy has a long lineage in the American experience. President Bush has made it clear that the war on terrorism is part of an idealistic historical mission that can be traced at least back to Harry Truman. American foreign policy under Bush was based upon "the ultimate goal of ending tyranny in our world" (Bush, 2006, 1). This bold idealism inspired the invasion of Iraq in 2003. The mythic quality of this ideal is obvious: since Plato, it is difficult to believe that tyranny can be ended.

The danger of looking to Truman as a model is that Truman made just the sorts of moral compromises in war that we should criticize. Truman's role in launching atomic bomb attacks against Japan led G.E.M. Anscombe to call him a murderer and a war criminal. Anscombe's critique focuses on the demand for unconditional surrender. This demand is part of the democratizing ideal: only when nondemocratic regimes have been radically changed, will the democratic project be actualized. But Anscombe notes that this sort of zeal for improvement caused Truman to justify murder. Anscombe uses Kantian language to condemn the bombings of Hiroshima and Nagasaki as nothing other than murder: "For men to choose to kill the innocent as a means to their ends is always murder" (Anscombe, 1981b, 64). Similar concerns led John Rawls to characterize Truman as a failed statesman (Rawls, 1999a, 99 ff.). In response to Rawls, Landesman has defended Truman's decision as a straightforwardly utilitarian one that made sense in the context of a global war against an undemocratic enemy committed to global domination at any price, that is, the Japanese (Landesman, 2003). Landesman goes on to claim that a statesman such as Truman has a responsibility to defend the lives of his own citizens—even if this means that he must discount the lives of innocent civilians on the other side.

Truman himself described his decision to use the atomic bombs in explicitly utilitarian terms. The question was how to force Japan to unconditionally surrender and so to begin moving Japan toward democracy in the postwar era. Truman wanted to accomplish this end while minimizing American casualties. Truman put it this way in an interview in 1955.

> They [the Japanese] never would have surrendered otherwise. I don't believe in speculating on the mental feeling and as far as the bomb is concerned I ordered its use for a military reason—for no other cause—and it saved the lives of a great many of our soldiers. That is all I had in mind. (Quoted in Ferrel, 2008, chapter 19)

This utilitarian reasoning was criticized by Douglas Lackey in his reply to Landesman. Lackey acknowledges the atrocities committed by the Japanese, including the Rape of Nanking. But Lackey reminds us that "the children who died at Hiroshima did none of those things" (Lackey, 2003, 42). Unless we are willing to discount the suffering of those on the other side—as Landesman does and as John Stuart Mill also did, as we shall see in a moment—we must remain committed to the deontological principle that innocent children should not be deliberately killed, even in pursuit of democratic and progressive ideals.

This discussion should remind us that when the democratizing myth is conjoined with utilitarianism it could lead us to make moral compromises. Utilitarians want efficient means to bring about good consequences. Rationalizations based on the idea that the end justifies the means are easier to make when we view the enemy through a lens that is tinged with racism or a sense of moral superiority. But we must remember that it is always wrong to deliberately kill children, whether Japanese, Iraqi, or the "barbarians" who were the "beneficiaries" of British colonial rule.

MILL'S PATERNALISM

One source for a utilitarian defense of the aggressive use of military force to spread democratic values and create peace is Mill's discussion of "non-intervention" in a short essay from 1859—an essay that has prompted responses by Walzer (1977, 86 ff.) and Chomsky (2007, 104 ff.). Mill's basic idea is that nonintervention among civilized nations is the best way to promote peace. Nonetheless, Mill allows for serious intervention in the affairs of noncivilized nations. Mill was writing a generation or more after "the Enlightenment" proper. Thus, Mill's ideas represent a development beyond the limits of the original idealism of the Enlightenment. Mill claims to develop his moral system in a way that is antithetical to Kant's. In chapter 1 of *Utilitarianism*, Mill claims that Kant failed, "almost grotesquely," to prove that there are contradictions in the maxims of those who hold "outrageously immoral" rules of conduct. So Mill announces that his approach is focused on outcomes and happiness and not on intentions or the rational test of noncontradiction that Kant formulated in the Categorical Imperative.

Nonetheless, Mill's effort to think about how to produce peace in international affairs follows closely upon ideas developed in the Enlightenment. One source for Mill's thinking about peace may be Bentham, who had articulated a theory of how to obtain perpetual peace at about the same time that Kant did. Bentham's utilitarian argument against war in his "A Plan for An Universal and Perpetual Peace" was originally written in 1789—5 years prior to the publication of Kant's essay. Bentham begins with the assumption that peace was profitable and that war produced unhappiness—an assumption that Mill for the most part agrees with. As Bentham put it at the beginning of his essay "Of War", "War is mischief upon the largest scale" (Bentham, 1843b, 544). Bentham's plan was more realistic than other similar plans—such as those of Rousseau or the Abbé Saint-Pierre. Bentham concentrated on a few simple principles and did not require the creation of a supranational organization. Rather, Bentham's proposal called for European Powers to relinquish their colonial holdings, since global competition was a source of animosity among Europeans. Mill also held that colonial possessions should be relinquished—but only after the colonies had reached a certain level of enlightenment.

Bentham proposed reducing the number of troops in the standing army, reducing the size of naval forces, and establishing an international tribunal to resolve disputes. Bentham advocated open and free trade. And, like Kant, he demanded that treaties and wars be conducted in the open without secrecy. He was not naïve enough to claim that this would be easily attainable. But his hope was to apply reason to the reality of war in order to reform political life and make way for the eventual end of war—especially war among the European powers. And for Bentham, this would be facilitated by progressive domestic politics in England and by a free and critical press that could make public the workings of power.

Mill picked up many of these ideas and developed them in the unique context of the mid-nineteenth century: a context in which England had abolished the slave trade and was gradually withdrawing from at least some of its colonial commitments. Nonetheless, Mill is still a product of his time; and his ideas reflect colonial bias and racial ideas. Mill was a member of the British establishment who benefited from colonial power in India and elsewhere. Some of the things that Mill says about "barbarians" in his essay on nonintervention as well as in *On Liberty* (both published in the same year—1859) indicate obvious Eurocentrism. In *On Liberty*, Mill says that political liberty is only a value for those who are civilized. For children and for human beings who are in their "nonage," despotism is justifiable. The same sorts of sentiments are expressed by Mill in his essay on nonintervention. Mill's racism reflects a sort of unthinking European supremacism that was quite common for a variety of important thinkers in the Western tradition including Hume, Kant, and Hegel.

Mill links his colonial racism to a utilitarian approach to progress and international affairs. The utilitarian argument would hold that as long as we are actually improving the barbarians in question through colonial intervention, we are promoting the greatest happiness for the greatest number. Not only are the barbarians themselves improved, but the spread of enlightenment will help to spread peace and international stability. Mill holds that there would be peace and international stability once nations respected the principle of nonintervention and learned to leave one another alone. Unfortunately, when we have barbarous neighbors who do not themselves accept such principles, then war remains a possibility. Indeed, Mill argues that interventions among barbarians are essential in order to establish conditions that would eventually make peaceful nonintervention possible (Mill, 1984, 119). Mill argues on utilitarian grounds both that forceful intervention would help to improve the lot of the barbarians by bringing them education and culture and that forceful intervention in the affairs of barbarian nations would also help in the long run to promote peace.

Now it is important to stress that, like Bentham, Mill saw that colonialism was not profitable in the long run. In his work, *Representative Government*, he argues that Great Britain's "colonies of European race" should be free. This argument is based upon the fact that the wars that were fought to keep the colonies in check were ultimately unprofitable. So Mill argues that "civilized" colonies should be left alone. However, for noncivilized peoples, Mill argues that "a vigorous despotism" is the best way of rendering them "capable of a higher civilization" (Mill, 1998b, 453). Again, Mill thinks that a benevolent despotism is the best way of cultivating civilized values among barbarians. And he argues that Great Britain would be such a benevolent despot precisely because it so values liberty.

This seems to be a contradiction: that despotism can be used as a means to promote liberty. But Mill's idea seems to have something in common with the Platonic ideal of a centralized authority who creates stability in order to promote and defend freedom. At any rate, Mill's benevolent despotism is aimed at reform and betterment of the people who are kept under paternal control. Ultimately, Mill maintains that when the colonies attain a sufficient level of enlightenment, they should be set free. We've already seen that Mill makes this sort of argument about the "colonies of European race." And when non-European people attain enlightenment, then freedom would be an option. But before that can happen, benevolent despotism must do its work. Mill further qualifies the idea of benevolent despotism by arguing that the colonial ruler should have a sort of independence from the mother country so that it can respond directly to the needs of the colony (as Mill thought happened in the case of the British East India Company). But in Mill's discussion of the needs of colonial government, we see the seed of a problem that has continually beset other well-intentioned interventions. Mill says, "A free country which attempts to govern a distant dependency, inhabited by a dissimilar people, by means of a branch of its own executive, will almost inevitably fail" (Mill, 1998b, 461). Mill's solution is to institute a better, more responsive sort of despotism. But it is a wonder that he did not hit upon the much more obvious solution: that colonial intervention itself and the project of forcing "civilization" upon a "barbarous" people is bound to be fraught with difficulty because the "barbarians" themselves will resent the intervention and will long to be free of their foreign governors. Unfortunately, Mill failed to recognize that liberty applies equally to all humans and that the liberty principle imposes a limit on forceful interventions, even among "barbarians."

THE KANTIAN IDEAL

Mill's goal of spreading civilization in order to create a stable international system of civilized nations appears to run counter to the means he proposed: it is odd to believe that liberty can be promoted by despotism. But utilitarians are not concerned about coordinating means and ends, in the way the deontologists are. Thus, Kant provides us with a response to Mill. Kant supplies us with the moral resources to resist the use of immoral means in pursuit of enlightenment and peace. Kant does defend the idea that peace will grow as democracy spreads. And he notes that wars can have progressive outcomes. But his critical perspective encourages us to avoid being seduced by the idea that we could use immoral means to produce progressive results. The goal of spreading enlightenment provides us with a regulative principle; but it should not be used as an excuse for immoral action.

There are three components of Kant's discussion of how peace should be obtained: a practical component that is related to the just war ideal, an institutional component that has to do with the way that deliberative democracy will act as a brake on war, and an international component articulated in terms of ideal of a federation of peaceful nations and the cosmopolitan idea of right. Beneath each of these is an emphasis on the basic framework of deontological ethics.

Kant articulated his vision of perpetual peace in terms of an international system of law, which would eventually eliminate war. But prior to the establishment of this ideal, Kant recognized that preliminary practical steps toward the ideal had to focus on the regulation of war according to ideas that have much in common with ideas of the just war tradition. His fifth "Preliminary Article" establishes a principle of nonintervention: "No state shall forcibly interfere in the constitution and government of another state" (Kant, 1991d, 96). And the sixth "Preliminary Article" identifies and prohibits a list of "dishonourable strategems." This list is quite similar to the principles of *jus in bello*: he prohibits assassination, use of poison, breaches of capitulation, and instigations of treason within war. These ideas were supported by arguing that restraint in warfare makes it more likely that we could conclude a war with a lasting and stable peace. The main part of Kant's essay argued that the goal of perpetual peace would require, in the long run, a league of nations—what Kant calls a "pacific federation" (*foedus pacificum*)—that would regulate and mitigate international hostility.

Recent interpreters of the Kantian idea—such as Doyle and Rawls—assume that democracies will not be externally aggressive, they will not fight expansive wars, and they have no interest in colonial or imperial power. But this interpretation also holds that democratic nations will be entitled to intervene in the affairs of nondemocratic peoples, under the general rubric of "humanitarian intervention." This idea fits better with Mill's discussion in his essay on "Non-Intervention" than with Kant's, since as noted above, Kant precludes intervention in the affairs of other nations. Aggressive wars aimed at historical change are not allowable in Kant's theory. Violent means, employed to spread democracy and peace, would lead to a contradiction in principle. Kant's moral philosophy, articulated in the idea of the categorical imperative, requires consistency among means and ends.

Kant's ideas can be traced back to the early eighteenth century and the Abbé de Saint-Pierre's *Project for Perpetual Peace*. Saint-Pierre's ideas were popularized by Rousseau as a sort of international confederation. A similar hope lay behind Leibniz's vision of uniting Europe in order to minimize war. Leibniz' project agreed, for the most part, with Saint-Pierre's. And Leibniz supplemented this with the dream of a common language that would unite Europe. As Rousseau indicated, the difficulty of such projects was the problem of persuading the princes or Europe to go along with them. Rousseau, however, found Saint-Pierre's idea untenable because politics was not governed by reason. Rousseau thus claims that the solution to war is not merely the use of reason and nonviolent means of persuasion; rather, it is the proper use of force. Unlike Rousseau, Kant is more hopeful about progress in history and about the application of reason in political life.

Kant's more inspiring idea is quite simply grounded in the liberal idea of citizen's rights. In *Perpetual Peace* Kant states that if people were asked to consent to war, they would be reluctant to consent; and most likely they would only consent to wars that were well justified. And in the *Rechtslehre*, Kant emphasizes that citizens must be asked to consent to war: "A citizen must always be regarded as a colegislative member of the state (that is not merely as a means, but at the same time as an end in itself), and as such he must give his free consent through his representatives, not only to the waging of war in general, but also to any particular declaration of war" (Kant, 1965b, 118). Morality requires that the people be asked if they are willing to go to war and willing to have their tax money used to support war—to do otherwise would be to use them merely as a means. But if people were asked, they would be reluctant to support war, since war would violate their own self-interest. The idea here is that self-interested individuals would generally not consent to war, if they are given the opportunity to consent.

Unfortunately, as Plato noted, this is not always true. It is possible to imagine self-interested people going to war to gain goods at the expense of the nation they conquer. And this is why Kant's idea also includes the idea of a pacific federation or a league of nations. Kant's deep systematic (or institutional) idea is that we really need what he calls in the *Rechtslehre*, a "universal union of states" (Kant, 1965b, 123). Such a global union would establish rules among nations in order to ensure peace. But in the *Rechtslehre*, Kant also notes that such an international state would be too large to govern; and thus he concludes that perpetual peace is "an idea that cannot be realized" (Kant, 1965b, 124). Instead, Kant argues that we should continually approach peace by gradually expanding a free and permanent congress of states whose members come together in order to ensure peace.

We might think that Kant's ideas provide a guide for proactive action in the way that the Bush Doctrine does. But Kant is reluctant to affirm such forceful expansion of democracy. Toward the end of his discussion of war in the *Rechtslehre*, Kant considers the very question of whether one could forcibly civilize savages and barbarians. He concludes that this would be wrong. Indeed, Kant maintains that warfare is itself an indication of savagery and barbarism. The very idea of the "Law of nations" is that nations should resolve their differences in a "civilized way by judicial process, rather than in the barbaric way of savages, namely, through war" (Kant, 1965b, 125). Kant goes on to question the right to conquest and colonization. He argues that there is "no right to colonize the land of another nation"; and he recognizes that foreign settlements "should not be undertaken through violence, but only through a contract" (ibid., 125, 126). Moreover, he considers whether colonization could be justified as a way of "bringing culture to primitive peoples." But he concludes that this would be unjust. In short, one should conclude from Kant's ideas that we cannot use violent means to spread democracy or enlightenment. This fits well with the moral idealism of the categorical imperative. We must be able to universalize our maxims; and a maxim of violent intervention would return upon the aggressor and undermine itself. Kant concludes his discussion in the *Rechtslehre*, as follows:

> No attempt should be made, however, to realize this idea precipitously through revolutionary methods, that is, by the violent overthrow of a previously existing imperfect and corrupt government . . . Instead, the idea should be attempted and carried out through gradual reform according to fixed principles. (Kant, 1965b, 129)

The problem with idealistic attempts to forcibly spread democracy in order to promote peace is that they fail to take seriously the sort of limit Kant recognizes here. Democracy should only be spread gradually through moral means. It should not be instituted by violent overthrow of the previously existing order.

CONCLUSION

An uncritical acceptance of the democratic peace ideal can lead to aggressive wars aimed to create democracy. When combined with the myth of the just war—the idea that it is easy to fight and win just wars—this idealism can become especially volatile. When utilitarian concerns that are not averse to using immoral means are combined with enlightenment idealism and colonialist and even racist ideas, then democratizing wars appear to be justifiable and it becomes easy to forgive deliberate atrocities committed as the means toward democratization. Indeed, immoral uses of violence committed in the name of democracy—from Truman's nuclear bombing of Japan to the American invasion of Iraq—can be justified by invoking utilitarian reasoning and the mythic ideal of the democratic peace. Ardent idealists who hope for perpetual peace can be seduced by the dark side of enlightenment, when the hope for historical transformation is divorced from deontological moral principles. The dark side becomes even more apparent when the hope for perpetual peace is linked either to ideas about teleology in history or about racial or cultural superiority. The antidote for all of this is a closer adherence to Kantian principles about justice. Kant hopes that the spread of republican principles in domestic politics and the growth of an international system will help to bring about perpetual peace. It is true that even Kant himself was susceptible to racist ideas. But the important point is that Kantian principles preclude expansive wars aimed at regime change in the name of democratization. And deontological ethics requires that when wars are fought as a reluctant last resort in defense of a just cause, they must be constrained by principles of discrimination that uniformly condemn the use of weapons of mass destruction.

CHAPTER SEVEN

THE VANITY OF TEMPORAL THINGS: HEGEL AND THE ETHICS OF WAR

War is that condition in which the vanity of temporal things and temporal goods takes on a serious significance.

Hegel, Philosophy of Right *(§ 324, Remark)*

The discussion of Kant and Mill in the last chapter pointed toward larger questions about history and progress. These sorts of questions are taken seriously by Hegel—a philosopher whose post-Enlightenment understanding of war was developed in response to the French Revolution and the Napoleonic wars of the early part of the nineteenth century. For Hegel, these events undermined the dream of enlightenment, as the "enlightened" revolution in France devolved into terror and imperial conquest. Unlike Kant and Mill, who were interested in thinking about war in moral terms, Hegel was more interested in the metaphysical question of what war shows us about human nature. And for Hegel, the answer is that war shows us the vanity of temporal things.

Hegel's insight appears to be similar to the idea expressed by Krishna in the *Bhagavad Gita*, where war exposes the fleeting nature of individuality. Hindu ideas did influence nineteenth century German philosophers such as Schopenhauer and Humboldt. In fact, Hegel knew Humboldt's work on Hinduism. But Hegel is no fan of Hinduism. Hegel thinks that Indian philosophy is nihilistic and that it ends up as "the freedom of the void," which "becomes . . . the fanaticism of destruction . . . " (Hegel, 1991, § 5). While Krishna uses war as a reminder that all things are fleeting, Hegel claims that war shows us that the state is more important than human individuality. In this sense, Hegel's "idealism" is quite similar to Platonic idealism: for both Hegel and Plato, the collective is more significant than the individual. Unlike Plato, however, Hegel inherits and approves of the liberal enlightenment idea of individual liberty. Thus, Hegel's theory is tragic: individual liberty and human autonomy are important values; however, in war individual autonomy can be sacrificed for the more substantial good of the state.

Hegel's view is foreshadowed in Kant's discussion of the sublimity of war. Indeed, Hegel's philosophical system revolves around sublime experiences and transformations. Hegel calls this "sublation" or "sublimation" (*aufhebung*). The idea is that war both cancels individuality and uplifts the individual at the same time. War lifts us to a larger perspective in which temporal things find their higher meaning. In his early lectures on "Natural Right and Political Science," Hegel maintains that war "shows the nothingness of particularity" (Hegel, 1995, § 160). War reminds us that particular goods such as individual life and even morality are limited goods that must be understood from within a larger context. While Hegel describes war as a condition that shows us the vanity of temporal things, the danger of Hegel's account is the corrosive effect that this has on attempts to defend moral limits on warfare.

HEGEL, HISTORICISM, AND THE JUST WAR TRADITION

The Hegelian idea that morality and individuality are limited goods is unacceptable to many. Kantians will claim that our duties are supposed to be universal and absolute. But Hegel claims that the Kantian view is limited: it is too abstract and formal to be meaningful. For Hegel, duty cannot be divorced from concrete historically grounded ethical and political life. And individuality only becomes meaningful when conceived in relation to the larger social whole. This means that deontological approaches to just war theory are insufficient from the Hegelian point of view. And it also means that "reasons of state" trump claims that are made on behalf of individuals.

States are, in Hegel's terms, individuals or totalities. Like Plato, Hegel held that individual human beings may be sacrificed—within limits—for the good of this larger sort of individual. Hegel's idea about sacrificing individuals for the good of the whole has made him a nemesis for liberals such as Karl Popper. Critiques of Hegel's political theory and his philosophy of war can also be found in the writings of Cassirer, Marcuse, Adorno, and others who traced the outlines of twentieth century totalitarianism in Hegel's thought. But unless one advocates both anarchism and pacifism, the Hegelian view will have to be taken seriously, since after all, we do sacrifice individuals to the state during war.

Hegel's approach has something in common with the just war tradition, especially with those who understand just war theory as part of a larger Christian theological doctrine aiming at a conception of the proper relation between Christian faith and political power. For Hegel, theological or spiritual interpretations of war remind us that morality and individuality are contained within a larger spiritual whole. Morality and individuality are not eliminated by adopting this larger perspective. Rather, the larger historical point of view shows us that these goods only exist within historically given forms of social life. Thus the state is the higher good that should be preserved even at the expense of sacrifices of individuality and moral purity. Christian just war theories might invoke the ideas of sin and grace in order to reconcile us to this compromise. But for Hegel, it is ultimately philosophy that provides for reconciliation to the tragic conflict between the whole and its parts. Hegel recognizes that human life contains alienation and apparent contradictions. The fact that we must make accommodations with "evil" indicates our finitude. We will be reconciled to this when we attain the philosophical purview in which evil and war are comprehended as part of the whole.

Hegel's ideas have been used (some would say, abused) by those who glorify war as a tool of social change. Ernst Cassirer once noted that the battle between German Fascists and Russian Communists in the Second World War could be described as a battle between Right- and Left-Hegelians (Cassirer, 1946, 249; see Holborn, 1943). Karl Popper condemned totalitarian violence of the sort typical of the twentieth century as a sort of "historicism" that he traced to Marx and Hegel. The idea that history has a *telos* can lead us to justify atrocities in the name of historical progress. Moreover, there is a tendency in Hegel to glorify war as both the crucible of historical change and the tonic that cures social ills. According to Popper, Hegel thought that "war is not a common and abundant evil but a rare and precious good" (Popper, 1971, vol. 2, 71). Hegel's basic idea about war, according to the critical approach of Cassirer and Popper, is that war is a means that can be employed in achieving the goal of history and that war is a good thing for the life of a nation. This critique of Hegel's ideas about war was concerned with the struggles of the mid-twentieth century between fascism, communism, and liberal-capitalism. Hegelian ideas resurfaced in the 1990s with Fukuyama's account of the "end of history" and in the general ideas of the "neoconservatives" who inspired the Bush Doctrine.

WAR AND TRAGEDY

It is an exaggeration to say that Hegel glorified war. But he did think that war was an integral part of political life (see Tyler, 2004). The Hegelian philosophy of war combines three elements: a realist description of international affairs, a critique of deonto-logical approaches to thinking about the morality of war, and an idealistic account of a historical destiny that superintends inter-national conflict. One of the implications of this approach is the idea that war shows us the transience of the finite and directs us toward higher goods. In this sense, war is beyond morality in an important and interesting way. Hegel thought that morality was, properly speaking, the concern of private individuals focused on the limited goods of private life. But since war involves much larger structures than mere individuality, it is beyond any simple sort of *moral* judgment. This is not to say that Hegel thinks that there are no limits to warfare. Indeed, Hegel does claim that such limits are created by the historical and cultural contexts in which wars are fought.

Hegel's approach to war developed as part of his understanding of the relation between religion, ethics, and political life. Hegel was aware of the differences between religious traditions with regard to warfare. He recognized that these differences were connected with the moral and political implications of religious truth. In his early work, "The Spirit of Christianity and Its Fate," Hegel notes that within the Christian tradition as developed in modern Europe, "war is not waged against the individual, but against the whole which lies outside him." This is contrasted with the Islamic tradition in which the individual is thought to contain the whole and in which, during war, "every single individual is put to the sword in the most cruel fashion" (Hegel, 1961, 260). Hegel seems to think that the developed Christian tradition represents progress beyond the Islamic notion

of jihad because it recognizes that the state is a spiritual formation that transcends individuality. With regard to limitations on
war in the European context, Hegel says that wars should "on no
account be waged either on internal institutions and the peace of
private and family life, or on private individuals" (Hegel, 1991, §
338). With this limitation, Hegel seems to reject both terrorism and
total wars, such as were fought throughout the twentieth century.
In his early lectures, he appears to reject wars "whose sole aim is
mutual destruction" (Hegel, 1995, § 163, Remark).

Nonetheless, even within the European tradition, states require
individuals to sacrifice themselves for the good of the nation during war. War thus turns ordinary morality on its head, whether
Christian or Kantian; and war calls many of our most cherished
values into question. It thus points beyond ethics and politics
toward the larger spheres of reconciliation found in art, religion,
and philosophy.

The charge that Hegel glorifies war can be traced to the fact
that Hegel thought that war was essential to the health of modern
nations because it helps to create patriotism and prevents nations
from sinking into the complacency and stagnation of peace. We
saw that Kant also maintained that peace can produce degeneracy
and effeminacy. But Hegel takes this idea and uses it to reject the
Kantian ideal of perpetual peace (Hegel, 1991, § 333, Remark; and
§ 324, Addition). The idea of a league of nations is at odds with the
modern idea of the nation state. Moreover, Hegel goes on to claim
that peace causes nations to become "stuck in their ways," "rigid
and ossified." Indeed, Hegel claims that even if there were peace, a
nation would need to "create an enemy" because wars strengthen
nations and because nations "gain internal peace as a result of wars
with their external enemies." Finally, war reminds individuals that
they have what Hegel calls a "universal duty" to sacrifice themselves for the good of the state (Hegel, 1991, § 325).

Hegel acknowledges that Kant thought that perpetual peace
was merely an ideal to be approached but not completed. In
Kant's language, it is an "ideal incapable of realization" (Kant
1991c, 171). According to Hegel's interpretation of Kant, it is an
"ideal toward which mankind should approximate" (Hegel, 1991,
§ 324, Addition). The difficulty for thinking about the morality
war is that the real world has not yet reached the condition of
perpetual peace. Short of the end of history in perpetual peace,

we must compromise with war. Indeed, we should also recognize that war has been an important force in historical progress. In his "Concluding Note" to his "Conjectures on the Beginning of Human History," Kant indicates that while war is horrible, it is also an "indispensable means" of spiritual progress (Kant, 1991a, 232). And even in *Perpetual Peace*, where he outlines a theory of justice in war (also developed in the *Metaphysics of Morals*), Kant indicates that nature uses war as a way of creating human progress (Kant, 1991d, 108–114). This includes stimulating the love of honor that is essential to human dignity, disseminating human culture around the globe, and even helping to develop the sense of international justice that is found in Kant's ideal. Hegel's ideas are thus not that far away from Kant's.

Hegel reminds us that Kantian morality alone is insufficient as a lens for considering war. But Hegel is not entirely opposed to thinking about morality in warfare. Rather, he locates the morality of war within the larger historical purview in which struggle, contradiction, and war are ubiquitous. Hegel's view has much in common with the Heraclitean philosophy we discussed in Chapter Two, since Hegel says that spirit is always at war with itself (Hegel, 1956, 55). Spirit is self-alienating activity that struggles with and against itself. In history, these struggles are manifest as war within and between different cultural structures of identity. Unlike Kant, Hegel's goal was not to articulate a path to perpetual peace. Rather, he wanted to find a way to reconcile us to war, despite its horrors, by locating war within a larger philosophical purview. Hegel's mature philosophy of war serves to reconcile us to history, not by proclaiming the end of war and the dawn of perpetual peace, but by showing us why war will continue to plague us and by accommodating morality to this fact.

In contemplating the destruction found in the history of spirit, we discover that spirit's self-identity is always, as Hyppolite puts it, fractured and tormented by "the negative." War thus shows us that life is tragic. Specifically it shows us that the identities and commitments of political life are fraught with peril since these identities are formed in opposition to other identities with which they will inevitably conflict. According to Hegel's view of war as a tragic conflict between political identity formations, such conflicts cannot be ethically mediated because ethical universals are entirely contained within a given political totality. For Hegel, the effect of tragedy, when properly understood, is not to eliminate conflict but to reconcile us to its ubiquity. War is a tragic conflict that cannot be reduced simply to questions of guilt or innocence, right or wrong.

In Hegel's most explicit consideration of war—in the discussion in the *Philosophy of Right*—Hegel discusses the ongoing *necessity* of war. This thesis is, basically, that political entities are dialectically related to other such entities in a struggle for mutual recognition. This struggle contains, at bottom, processes that are famous from Hegel's analysis of the master-slave dialectic in the *Phenomenology of Spirit*. The master-slave dialectic is the focus of interpreters of Hegel such as Kojève and Fukuyama. However, in the realm of politics as Hegel conceives it in the *Philosophy of Right*, there is no explicit hope for a lasting structure of mutual recognition that would resolve the differences between political entities. The reason for this is quite simple: there is no sovereign power to unite the differences that exist between different states. The international struggle for recognition is thus a structural necessity.

This structural realism seems to be in contradiction with Hegel's ideas about "the end of history" as emphasized by Kojève's and Fukuyama's interpretation of Hegel. Fukuyama's thesis that liberal values will triumph through the historical struggle for recognition is an adequate interpretation of the early Hegel. This interpretation is especially useful when applied to developments *within* a national or cultural form of life, that is, when applied to the European context. However, it is doubtful that in international affairs any final stage of mutual recognition is possible. Thus, a "clash of civilizations" in Huntington's sense may ensue, especially when we hold out the possibility that different "civilizations" (what Hegel calls in the *Philosophy of Right*, "world-historical realms") will resolve their own "internal" struggles for recognition in different ways (Hegel, 1991, § 354). This interpretation reflects Hegel's more mature view as developed in the *Philosophy of Right*.

Although Kojève, Fukuyama, and others emphasize the goal of mutual recognition found in Hegel's *Phenomenology*, even in the *Phenomenology* Hegel calls into question the process by which war creates spiritual progress. Hegel writes that war is a limited mechanism precisely because it is physical and not spiritual. "Now, it is physical strength and what appears as a matter of luck that decides on the existence of ethical life and spiritual necessity"

(Hegel, 1977, 289). Wars are won or lost because of contingencies: economics, weather, geography, and just plain luck. This problem is revisited in the *Philosophy of History* where we find that spiritual progress uses the finite and the physical to develop its idea through history. Part of the meaning of the so-called cunning of reason in Hegel's philosophy of history is that spiritual development occurs via luck and contingency. While other forms of realism acknowledge such contingencies, Hegel spiritualizes them and holds out the hope that spirit uses these contingencies to bring about progress. War reminds us of the importance of contingency and the physical in the political realm. War shows us that we need to adopt a larger perspective to make sense of a world in which physical contingencies produce spiritual progress.

HEGEL IN HISTORICAL CONTEXT

As mentioned above, Hegel's view of war was articulated in response to Kant. Hegel was also reacting to Hobbes and Rousseau. And his ideas should be understood in the context of nineteenth century history which included the Napoleonic wars. To begin, it is important to note that Hegel's explicit rejection of Rousseau's notion of the social contract informs his view of the duty that citizens have to sacrifice themselves for the state during war (Hegel, 1991, § 258, Remark). For Hegel, the idea of the social contract cannot account for the demands that the state makes upon individuals. The fact that individuals sacrifice themselves for the state in war shows us that the state has a kind of majesty that cannot be reduced to a social contract. Rousseau also distinguishes the properly *political* meaning of war from the state of personal enmity and ubiquitous violence that Hobbes called "war" in chapter 13 of the *Leviathan* or chapter 1 of *De Cive* where he describes the state of nature as a condition of war that is of all men against all men (*bellum omnium contra omnes*). As Rousseau explains, "War, then, is not a relation between man and man, but a relation between State and State, in which individuals are enemies only by accident, not as men, nor even as citizens, but as soldiers; not as members of the fatherland, but as its defenders. In short, each State can have as enemies only other States and not individual men, inasmuch as it is impossible to fix any true relation between things of different kinds" (Rousseau, 1967, 13–14). Hegel agrees that states and war cannot be understood as merely relations between "man and man." Rather, the state is an entity that has a being that transcends human individuals and war shows us this directly.

Rousseau's contractarian perspective leads to the idea of limited warfare. Rousseau argues, for example, for noncombatant immunity: a declaration of war does not justify the killing of those who are not employed as soldiers. Declarations of war are warnings given to the citizens of the nation that is declared to be the enemy (Rousseau, 1967, 14). The warning says that if citizens of the enemy state take up arms, they may be killed by the soldiers of the state declaring the war. Connected with this is the correlative right to surrender: when enemy soldiers lay down their arms, they are no longer acting as soldiers and thus ought not to be killed. Rousseau connects his thinking about war with the master-slave relation in a way that resonates with Hegel. For Rousseau, the "master" has no right to kill the "slave" because enmity should end once one party gives up its arms. But without the right to kill the "slave," the "master" has no power over him. Thus the master-slave relation is at best an unstable cease-fire that it is not actually a state of peace (Rousseau, 1967, 15).

Hegel fills in the details of this in the *Phenomenology* by arguing that the way to overcome the master-slave dialectic is to move toward a higher level of mutual recognition found in the state. While the master-slave dialectic helps to explain the necessity of the social compact, it poses an interesting problem for international relations. If states are involved in a struggle for mutual recognition, as Hegel claims in the *Philosophy of Right*, but if there can be no lasting mutual recognition between states, because there is no sovereign power over them, as Hegel also suggests, then international relations cannot reach a peaceful conclusion. Thus, while Hegel follows Rousseau at the level of domestic politics, he leaves us with something like a Hobbesian view at the level of international politics. This follows from Hegel's understanding of political identity. In the realm of politics, it is states that are sovereign individuals. These sovereign individuals cannot give up their sovereignty without losing their own individuality. Although Hegel does argue that finite human persons find their individuality completed in the state, states themselves cannot be transcended in this way. And there is no way to resolve the struggle between these political "individuals" other than war.

Hegel, then, like Hobbes, can be considered as a "realist" with regard to international relations. Hegel does not agree with the liberal idealism of Kant. Kant explicitly argued against a Hobbesian approach to international affairs. Kant wanted war to be conducted according to principles of justice in war with the ultimate goal of bringing an end to war. Kant also envisioned a supranational league of nations. For Hegel, this is a utopian dream that runs counter to the truth of political life, which is that states are sovereign individuals who cannot cede their sovereignty to an international institution without giving up their very identity.

We might think that Hegel shares with his contemporary, Carl von Clausewitz, the view that war is "a continuation of policy by other means" (Clausewitz, 1982, 119). Clausewitz and Hegel were social acquaintances in Berlin and they both died in 1831. Clausewitz's essays were not published until after his death in 1832, so Hegel would not have had access to Clausewitz's published thoughts on war. At any rate, Clausewitz means that war always has a political objective and that the nature of this objective should help give shape to the means employed. Limitations on warfare, according to Clausewitz, are derived from and proportional to the political goals of war. Hegel would most likely agree with this assessment. But Hegel incorporates the theory of war as a political instrument in a much broader context that is concerned with the ontology of the state and the teleology of history. Like Clausewitz, however, Hegel thought that ideas about warfare needed to develop in concert with technological development and ultimately had to cohere with the political ideas that guided warfare.

Clausewitz thought that Napoleon was a genius for actualizing the new political ideal of France in military form: by using the mass army. And he recognized that Napoleon had evolved a new form of democratic warfare that moved away from the stylized battles of the eighteenth century. Hegel also celebrated Napoleon. Hegel saw Napoleon in person at Jena in 1806 as he was completing his *Phenomenology of Spirit*. He described Napolean as the "world-soul" on horseback (see Pinkard, 2001, 228). But Hegel also recognized that despite Napoleon's military prowess, "never was the powerlessness of victory exhibited in clearer light" because Napoleon's victories alone were unable to disseminate and expand the spiritual ideas of the age (Hegel, 1956, 451). Napoleon's failures demonstrate that war alone is insufficient as an instrument of progress.

Like Clausewitz, Hegel thought that new political arrangements and new technology required new ways of understanding war. In one interesting passage, Hegel writes that the invention of the gun "has turned the purely personal form of valour into a more abstract form" (Hegel, 1991, § 328, Remark). In other words, modern warfare has become abstract insofar as modern technology depersonalizes warfare. As Hegel explains in the *Philosophy of History*, gunpowder neutralizes the force of mere physical strength (Hegel, 1956, 402). It is no longer the strong arm that prevails. Rather, gunpowder creates conditions in which intelligence, generalship, character, and "unity of spirit" are more essential for determining the outcome of warfare. For Hegel, all of this is contained in the idea that wars are understood in a broad context that comprehends politics, science, and technology.

WAR AND IDEAS

Wars are clashes of ideas that help people clarify their values as they unite in opposition to a common foe. Hegel indicates, for example, that the Trojan War had this effect on the Greeks, just as the Crusades served to unite Christendom during the Middle Ages (Hegel, 1956, 230–231). And he discusses how the wars against the Turks united the European family of nations (ibid., 432–433). Wars can also bring forth new eras of world-historical significance. The Greeks' victory over Persia is interpreted by Hegel as the triumph of the principle of freedom against the principle of despotism (ibid., 257). While some of this reflects a Romanticized view of the Greeks and Hegel's Eurocentric view of history, there is something plausible about the idea that wars are fought in the name of ideas and that there can be wars that are regarded as progressive in this sense (see Fiala, 2002a). Progressive wars are those that helped to develop the notion of freedom, such as the wars of religion in the seventeenth century or the French Revolution. But Hegel's ambivalence toward the French Revolution and its excess shows us the sense of Hegel's philosophy of war: war might be necessary and progressive but nonetheless terrible.

In the realm of politics where there are dialectically differentiated political identities, war is often the only recourse when these identities come into conflict. These identity conflicts are not only focused on states, they also include religious differences. Such ideological warfare is a necessary part of the development of ideas in history. Hegel says of the Thirty Years War, for example, that it was "indispensable to the security of Protestants" (Hegel, 1956, 434). And in England, "war was indispensable to the establishment of the Protestant church" (ibid., 435). It is interesting to note (especially in light of our current war on terrorism) that in this conflict, Hegel claims that the people were "fanatical"—basing their will to fight on religious faith (ibid., 435). This is significant because it indicates a further point of tragedy: that fighters on each side can be entirely convinced of the righteousness of their cause.

These religious wars involved a clash of absolutes—in Hegel's language they were based upon "absolute mistrust": "absolute, because mistrust bound up with the religious conscience was its root" (Hegel, 1956, 434). Hegel thus recognizes that religious and ideological differences can lead to war and that war cannot be reduced merely to self-interest narrowly conceived. Indeed, Hegel's interpretation of the French Revolution and the Napoleonic wars conceives of these events as political attempts to export philosophical ideas. However, Hegel claims that this was destined to fail because "it is false that the fetters which bind Right and Freedom can be broken without the emancipation of conscience—that there can be Revolution without a Reformation" (ibid., 453). Individual nations must develop, on their own terms and at their own pace, toward the idea of freedom. Although wars can be fought in defense of ideas, ultimately war alone is insufficient to bring about progress. Genuine spiritual development is also necessary.

War facilitates spiritual development by reminding us of the vanity of temporal things. War makes the sublation of individuality that we find in religion palpable for us. In Hegel's language, war demands the "sacrifice" (*Aufopferung*) of individual persons: their property, their happiness, and their very lives (Hegel, 1991, § 324). It is significant that this is the same language that Hegel uses to describe religious devotion. Hegel recognizes that political patriotism and religious devotion are quite similar. In his discussion of this similarity in the *Philosophy of History* he says: "By sacrifice (*Opfer*) man expresses his renunciation of his property, his will, his individual feelings" (Hegel, 1956, 49). The sacrifices of war thus have a religious connection. At least, war is about ideas and interests that are more important than individual property, happiness, and even life.

Hegel's view is important because it reminds us of the spiritual basis of war, that is, a basis that transcends individual self-interest and material need. Individuals do sacrifice their lives and property for ideas. The demand that some individuals sacrifice their lives in defense of an idea only makes sense if this sacrifice is about spiritual values that transcend the immediate economic interests of the finite individual. With this in mind, it is easy to see why Hegel rejects the Kantian thesis that the spread of republican values will produce perpetual peace. Kant's emphasis on individual consent devolves to a focus on material self-interest; and this fails to account for the power or majesty of the state. Even though it is possible for there to be international agreement about the principles of political right, Hegel seems to think that liberal nations might still go to war with one another, if only because their political identities are always involved in the mutual struggle for recognition (Hegel, 1991, § 339, Addition). What drives a nation to war is its interest in being recognized by others (ibid., §§ 334–336). These national interests cannot be reduced to the material interests of individuals in a way that might give support to the Kantian view. Moreover, without an international sovereign who might resolve potential conflicts, Kant's further idea about instituting a federation of nations is useless (Hegel, 1991, § 324, Addition; and § 259, Addition).

CONCLUSION

Hegel's approach to the philosophy of war has much in common with the way that war is understood in Platonic philosophy and in Greek tragedy: Hegel accepts war as a part of the social world and attempts to deal with it as such. A philosophy of war, in Hegel's sense, must link the contingencies of physical nature, fate, and luck with the necessary logical development of spirit in history. Hegel's philosophy of history and politics develops as a dialectic between tragic conflicts and their philosophical reconciliation. War shows us that there are tragic conflicts about ideas and identities. These conflicts push us toward a realization of the transience of finite things, including perhaps toward a recognition of the transience of nations and states themselves.

This move beyond politics toward religion can seem to be spiritually fulfilling: a nation at war needs a higher sense of reconciliation in which the sacrifices of war are redeemed as reasons of state.

The worry about this religious turn in thinking about war is that it allows us to ignore the suffering of war by claiming that spirit is actualizing itself on the slaughter-bench of history. But this critique applies to any approach to the morality of war that strays beyond deontological prohibitions and is willing to consider consequences, proportionality, and the possible historical necessity of supreme emergency exemptions. In the complex world beyond abstract deontological commandments and private moral purity, we are faced with difficulty judgments of historical import involving the life and death of individuals and nations. The danger of straying beyond deontology is that we may end up justifying atrocity in the name of historical destiny as did those "historicists" who were inspired by Hegel. To resist this slippage, we must recall that Hegel thought that there were limitations in modern warfare, even if these limitations were culturally and historically located. This is a sort of relativism: Hegel's approach takes seriously the idea that change occurs in political ideas and in technological capacity. But Hegel also acknowledges that deontological morality continues to be one of the ideas that "we"—by which Hegel means, modern enlightened Europeans—must reconcile ourselves to. The virtue of Hegel's approach is that he recognizes the power of war to reduce our most cherished values to nothing. A critic may contend that this is precisely why war should be abolished. But Hegel reminds us that until history ends, we will have to reconcile ourselves to the vanity of temporal things that is exposed in war.

CHAPTER EIGHT

AMERICAN AMBIVALENCE: MILITARISM, PACIFISM, AND PRAGMATISM

I have nothing, had nothing, and have nothing now to say directly about the war.

John Dewey, December 7, 1941

We've seen that Hegelian idealism can lead to a sort of admiration for war. After Hegel, this idealism became increasingly militant. There was a general fascination with power among writers at the end of the nineteenth century, from the Social Darwinists to Nietzsche and on to the fascists of the twentieth century. Nietzsche, for example, seemed to think that war was a necessary and healthy process. In the *Will to Power*, Nietzsche writes that peace is contrary to the laws of biology and that "life is a consequence of war, society itself a means to war" (Nietzsche, 1968, 33). These ideas became part of an ideology of militarism that celebrated military power as beneficial and war itself as salutary. The militarist ideal holds that the state is primary and that the life of the professional soldier is admirable and even superior to the life of ordinary civilians. Often this was combined with racist and colonial attitudes such as we saw in our prior discussion of Kant and Mill. Militarism flourished in the early part of the twentieth century, leading to imperialistic wars that culminated in the horrors of the two World Wars.

Today some critics have refocused our attention on what Andrew Bacevich calls, "the new American militarism":

Americans have fallen prey to militarism, manifesting itself in a romanticized view of soldiers, a tendency to see military power as the truest measure of national greatness, and outsized expectations regarding the efficacy of force. (Bacevich, 2005, 2)

The resurgence of militarism in the United States should lead us to reconsider historic discussions of militarism in America's indigenous philosophical tradition: from Emersonian Transcendentalism to the pragmatist school of the early twentieth century. The problem for American pragmatism is that war is itself an indictment of the philosophical presumption that the world is a reasonable place. John Dewey seems to reflect this fact in his comments on the day that the Japanese attacked Pearl Harbor. Dewey was scheduled to give a talk entitled, "Lessons from the War in Philosophy," when Pearl Harbor was attacked (Dewey, 1988). Dewey made the remarks quoted as the epilogue for this chapter and then proceeded with his planned lecture, which had nothing to do with Pearl Harbor. As an old philosopher—by now 82 years old—who had survived the intellectual tumult of the First World War, Dewey appeared to have realized that war posed a problem for philosophy. Indeed, the problem is that the world does not cooperate with our best-laid plans. A war aimed at a good cause can go awry; and the productive social energy of warfare can be corrupted toward militarism.

AMBIVALENCE IN THE AMERICAN TRADITION

Even before the Civil War, Americans condemned militarism. In his indictment of American military power and military service in "Civil Disobedience," Thoreau said that "the mass of men serve the state thus, not as men mainly, but as machines." For Thoreau, the problem is that the "wooden men" who make up the "standing army" are esteemed as "good citizens," while the real heroes are the men of conscience—individuals who resist the centralizing and brutalizing aspects of military power.

However, despite a basic commitment to peace and to individuality, American philosophers sometimes accommodated war and praised centralized political power. Thoreau supported abolitionist violence; Emerson praised Lincoln for Northern victory in the Civil War; and Dewey and Royce both supported American involvement in the Great War. Pacifism runs deep in the American tradition: from the Quakers who founded Pennsylvania to Jane Addams, Martin Luther King, Jr., and Cesar Chavez. At the same time, however, American philosophers also recognize that there is power in collective action and perhaps even virtue in warfare. And American political leaders such as Teddy Roosevelt developed the ideals of Transcendentalism in a militarist direction.

It may seem odd that Transcendentalism can be developed into militarism—since transcendental contemplation seems antithetical to the chaos of war. But Emerson and Thoreau were themselves ambivalent about war. Emerson and Thoreau supported the Civil War and even the idea of using terrorism to free the slaves. While viewing war primarily as an affront to individuality, Emerson and Thoreau approved of the "terrorism" of Capt. John Brown, the abolitionist who attacked Harper's Ferry in hope of creating a slave rebellion. Some consider Brown to be an American terrorist—not only for his raid on Harper's Ferry but for his participation in the Pottawattamie Creek Massacre. But Emerson praised Brown as "a pure idealist, with no by-ends of his own." Thoreau praises Brown as a "transcendentalist above all, a man of ideas and principles . . . not yielding to a whim or transient impulse, but carrying out the purpose of a life" (Thoreau, 2000a, 720–721). While Emerson and Thoreau thought Brown was a virtuous, self-reliant man intrepidly pursuing justice, he was also a fanatic who used violence in pursuit of his idea of justice.

The issue here is whether it is right to utilize extreme violence in the name of a higher good. In his essay, "War" (from 1838), Emerson echoes Kant in calling for us to overcome war. However, Emerson also understood the importance of fighting for the abolition of slavery. And he ultimately supported the Civil War. In the same way, although Thoreau's essay "Civil Disobedience" specifically criticizes the Mexican war and the more general way that militarism dehumanizes us, he too thought that violence could be appropriate in the cause of abolition.

Moreover, the Transcendentalists were fascinated by manly strength, courage, and tenacity. In the essay, "War," Emerson states that the chief attraction of war is that it calls for the virtues of self-reliance. In war, we are thrown back upon ourselves and discover that we cannot ask for protection from anyone other than ourselves. War, for Emerson, was thus understood as the historical crucible in which self-reliance was formed. In "War," Emerson writes: "This self-subsistency is the charm of war; for this self-subsistency is essential to our idea of man" (Emerson, 1911c, 173). However,

Emerson imagines that we can now evolve beyond the need for war as the mechanism that develops self-reliance. "The manhood that has been in war must be transferred to the cause of peace, before war can lose its charm, and peace be venerable to men" (ibid., 171). This theme will return again in ideas expressed by Jane Addams, William James, and Josiah Royce.

Emerson's understanding of heroism can help explain his admiration for John Brown. Emerson's self-reliant individual can seem fanatical. However, Emerson seems to believe that the truly self-reliant individual will ultimately be in tune with justice. Brown was, according to Emerson, a man of utmost "integrity, truthfulness, and courage" whose primary values were grounded in the Golden Rule and in the Declaration of Independence (Emerson, 1911b, 269–270, 268). Emerson was outraged that the state of Virginia would execute a hero in the cause of abolition; and he admired Brown's courage in pursuit of abolition. The true hero is single-minded and self-reliant, courageous and persistent, and in step with the just demands of his time. In this regard Emerson praised Lincoln as follows: "There, by his courage, his justice, his even temper, his fertile counsel, his humanity, he stood a heroic figure in the center of a heroic epoch" (Emerson, 1911a, 335). Although this sort of heroism should eventually develop beyond the need for war, Emerson thought that the evil of slavery required heroic and violent action.

The abolition of slavery could provide a serious and compelling reason to support war—even for those who were opposed to state power and to the grinding, depersonalizing nature of militarism. The Civil War may be understood as an obvious case of a just war: if it is conceived primarily as an effort to abolish slavery and not merely as a federalist power grab. Nonetheless, atrocities occurred during this war—including Sherman's "march to the sea" and the strategy of "total war." Sherman used the phrase "war is cruelty" in his letter to Atlanta on September 12, 1864. He subsequently burned the city to the ground. Sherman also claimed that "fear is the beginning of wisdom." This explained the Northern strategy: to force the Rebels into submission by destroying cities and farmland. After the Civil War, Americans had to come to terms with the fact that atrocities were committed, even in pursuit of the just cause of abolition.

Philosophers in the American tradition thus tend to recognize a deep ambivalence in human nature. We are at once warlike and peace loving. We value the individual but also benefit from the power of communal action. We admire heroism and the strenuous life of the warrior, while also valuing stoic retreat and transcendental contemplation. War brings out the best and the worst of human nature. It creates opportunities for virtues such as loyalty and courage; but it also results in death and destruction.

TURN-OF-THE-CENTURY IMPERIALISM AND ANTI-IMPERIALISM

We find ambivalence about war in American philosophy at the turn of the twentieth century. This was a time in which the United States was expanding its power through imperialistic military adventures that were justified by the ideology of what Kipling called the "white man's burden." The Civil War began a process through which stat and military power expanded in the name of justice and civilization. From the Indian Wars and the subjugation of Native Americans to the annexation of Hawaii to wars in Cuba and the Philipines, American power was understood as part of a righteous civilizing mission. But American power also expanded in pursuit of money and land. The duplicitous nature of American power disgusted critics such as Mark Twain. Consider, for example, Twain's "War Prayer" (from 1905). Twain describes a patriotic crowd praying for victory. But a lunatic prophet interrupts the rally to explain that in praying for victory, they are actually praying for God to create the dismembered bodies of the enemy along with their grieving widows and fatherless children. Twain's message is that the desire for power and victory and righteousness causes us to turn a blind eye to the human suffering of war.

Ambivalence about war in American philosophy reflects the duplicitous nature of American power and politics. Americans—especially white businessmen—benefited from war and conquest, while the American ideology proclaimed a commitment to peace, equality, and liberty. American power expanded by warfare throughout the past centuries, while often masking power in the ideals of the Declaration of Independence. While espousing ideals of life, liberty, and happiness, American war-making has routinely been tinged with racism and imperialistic swagger: from the Indian Wars to racially charged imperialistic adventures in the Pacific, from the genocidal "trail of tears" to Japanese internment camps during the Second World War.

American philosophy appears to be committed to peace, while American political life has developed through war. This ambivalence was explained by John Dewey at the dawn of the First World War as reflecting the fact that the American people are both "profoundly pacifist" and aware of the power of "military participation" (Dewey, 1993b, 195 and 196). Dewey's claim about American pacifism seems to fit the American people into the paradigm of the Kantian dream of peace-loving democracies. But American history gives us a reason to doubt what we might call "the myth of American pacifism." Americans are committed to ideals of equality and liberty, while the wars we fight have racial and imperialistic overtones. The American state is conceived in colonial violence. It is born in revolution and matures through a bloody civil war. And then the American state achieves hegemony through the wars of the twentieth century. The myth of American pacifism runs aground on the reality of American militarism.

The philosophers in the American tradition struggled to make sense of these sorts of conflicting values. William James, for example, came of age during the American Civil War—a war that touched his own family directly and caused him to question his own courage (see Menand, 2002, chapter 4). James was personally frustrated by his own ambivalence about the war. But this ambivalence is rooted in a fundamental conflict of values. The cause of abolition seems a good one; but is war the best or only solution? James ambivalence is symptomatic of the American philosophical view. In recognizing moral complexity and value pluralism, it becomes quite difficult to justify war.

James' essay, "The Moral Equivalent of War" (from 1906), may be the most famous and explicit expression of this sort of ambivalence. The gist of this essay is that we need to evolve beyond war while finding a way to preserve the virtues developed in war. James hated war. But he also reluctantly agreed with militarists such as Teddy Roosevelt that war was productive of the masculine virtues of the strenuous life. Roosevelt explicitly praised the strenuous life of the warrior, and favored the idea of carrying a "big stick." Roosevelt, for example, argued in 1897 when he was Secretary of the Navy that "preparation for war is the surest guarantee of peace" and that "peace is a goddess only when she comes with sword girt on thigh" (Roosevelt, 1897). And in his speech on "The Strenuous Life" (first delivered in 1899), Roosevelt praised the "iron in the blood" of Lincoln and other American warriors, while mocking weaklings, cowards, and pacifists. "The timid man, the lazy man, the man who distrusts his country, the over-civilized man, who has lost the great fighting, masterful virtues . . . these are the men who fear the strenuous life . . . they believe in that cloistered life which saps the hardy virtues in a nation, as it saps them in the individual" (Roosevelt, 1905b, 7–8). Roosevelt continued to mock what he called "ultrapacifists" in his reflection on the World War. He did propose a practical solution to conflict—by way of a league of nations along the lines of Wilson (and Kant). But for Roosevelt, genuine peace requires righteousness. Thus, Roosevelt complained that the ultrapacifists give up on justice in the name of peace. On the eve of the First World War, Roosevelt wrote: "Only mischief has sprung from the activities of the professional peace prattlers, the ultrapacifists, who, with the shrill clamor of eunuchs, preach the gospel of the milk and water of virtue and scream that belief in the efficacy of diluted moral mush is essential to salvation" (Roosevelt, 1915, 244). Roosevelt's masculine and militaristic vision of the world was typical of the worldview of the end of the nineteenth and early-twentieth centuries.

For Americans, the end of the nineteenth century was marked by a profound shift from the struggle to tame the frontier to the effort to enter the great game of global politics. Frontier individualism and the wilderness experience seemed to inspire Teddy Roosevelt and the ideal of the strenuous life. Indeed, the link between Roosevelt and the Transcendentalists can be made by way of America's greatest defender of wilderness, John Muir. Muir was inspired by Emerson, whom he met when Emerson visited Yosemite. And Muir also entertained Teddy Roosevelt when he came to Yosemite. Some have argued that it was the closing of the frontier that led Americans overseas in pursuit of land, fortune, and adventure under Roosevelt and his contemporaries. Indeed, Frederick Jackson Turner argued that with the closing of the American frontier, American "energies of expansion" would lead to "the demands for a vigorous foreign policy, for an interoceanic canal, for a revival of our power upon the seas, and for the extension of American influence to outlying islands and adjoining countries" (Turner, 1896). Turner's prophecy came true under McKinley and Roosevelt.

Roosevelt and the American imperialists defended these "energies of expansion" as necessary to the health of the nation.

Roosevelt praised President Grant, for example, for recognizing that when confronted with the choice between shrinking or expanding, Grant chose to expand. "Grant saw to it that we did not shrink, and therefore we had to expand when the inevitable moment came" (Roosevelt, 1905a, 223). Roosevelt claimed that Grant embodied the ambivalence of the American tradition along with Washington and Lincoln. These great leaders "were men who, while they did not shrink from war, were nevertheless heartily men of peace" (ibid., 209). Roosevelt concluded that strong men must embrace the strenuous life and necessity of war.

Given the manly virtues praised by Roosevelt and other militarists, it is not surprising, then, that an alternative would be articulated by a woman. While Roosevelt belittled the ultrapacifists as "eunuchs," Jane Addams offered a genuine feminist alternative. Addams foreshadows the ideas that James developed in his essay on the moral equivalent of war. Addams said, for example, in a speech from 1899:

> Let us not make the mistake of confusing moral issues sometimes involved in warfare with warfare itself. Let us not glorify the brutality. The same strenuous endeavor, the same heroic self-sacrifice, the same fine courage and readiness to meet death, may be displayed without the accompaniment of killing our fellow men. (Addams, 2005a, 3)

Addams goes on to single out Kipling and his idea of the "white man's burden" for failing to distinguish between war and the advance of civilization. For Addams, as for James, war and imperialism are simply not the best method for making progress.

Addams and James both recognize the need for forms of social organization that provide alternatives to militarism and war. Addams was actively involved in creating these alternatives through her work at Hull House and her work with the Women's International League for Peace and Freedom. Both Addams and James recognize that war will remain a social and political fact until we are able to evolve beyond that sort of idealism that sees virtue in the brutality of war. Moreover, they both understood that the ideology of militarism was disseminated by a class of professional soldiers and political leaders who used that ideology to gain power at the expense of the rest of society. James worries that what he calls "the professional military class" is clinging to war and refusing to admit that "war may be a transitory phenomenon in social evolution" (James, 1987, 1284). The key for critics of the war machine was to push social evolution in a more humane and more peaceful direction.

While the Spanish-American War stimulated the critical thought of both James and Addams, the atrocities of the subsequent Philippine-American war further inspired antiwar and anti-imperialist criticism. Prominent members of the Anti-Imperialist League, which opposed the horrors the Philippine War, included Mark Twain, William Jennings Bryan, as well as James and Addams (in the central branch in Chicago). Roosevelt's militarism led Mark Twain to claim that Roosevelt was "clearly insane . . . and insanest upon war and its supreme glories" (cited in Watt, 2003, 1). Twain's anti-imperialism was directed at the whole ideology that was linked to the idea of the white man's burden. In his essay "To the Person Sitting in Darkness," Twain explained his opposition to mission-ary interventions abroad that purported to bring light to those who were "sitting in darkness" in China, the Philippines, Cuba, and elsewhere. Toward the end of that essay, Twain quipped that in the Philippines the American flag should be redesigned to include the skull and crossbones. Imagining himself as a recipient of American imperial intervention, Twain explained the apparent contradiction in American ideals and policy as follows:

There is something curious about this—curious and unaccount-able. There must be two Americas: one that sets the captive free, and one that takes a once-captive's new freedom away from him, and picks a quarrel with him with nothing to found it on; then kills him to get his land. (Twain, 1992c, 467)

This sort of contradiction led William James to decry what he called the "murder" of Philippine culture, concluding, "God damn the U.S. for its vile conduct in the Philippine Isles" (quoted in Zinn, 2005, 315). Twain and James both interpreted American militarism as a deadly combination of greed and militarism. Twain's "Battle Hymn of the Republic (Brought Down to Date)" claimed that with "the orgy of the launching of the sword," "lust is marching on" and "greed is marching on" (Twain, 1992a, 474–475).

Opponents of imperialism like Twain, Addams, and James were apparently the timid pacifists that Teddy Roosevelt mocked.

Roosevelt claimed that such "men" hid their timidity behind pacifism and humanitarianism in order to "excuse themselves for the unwillingness to play the part of men" (Roosevelt, 1905b, 19). While James may have been interested in preventing the destruction of indigenous Philippine culture because of his recognition of value pluralism, Roosevelt would have thought that such an argument was absurd. Indeed, in "The Strenuous Life," Roosevelt linked the war in the Philippines to the civilizing mission of the state—a mission that included the need to continually work to civilize the Indians of North America.

James' disgruntled reaction against American imperialism provoked some reaction among the philosophical community. James' colleague at Harvard, George Santayana, offered a somewhat cynical analysis of James' anti-imperialism. According to Santayana, James was suffering from disillusionment: James felt that he had "lost his country" when the United States annexed the Philippines (Santayana, 1986, 402). For Santayana, the problem of the Philippines was not American aggression and strength but, rather, Spanish weakness—a claim that belies Santayana's resigned acknowledgment of the way that power works in the world. Santayana complained that James held a "false moralistic view of history," which maintained that politics should be subject to moral principles and that political actors should be viewed as responsible agents with free will (ibid., 403). Santayana rejected this view. Instead, for Santayana, political agents are "creatures of circumstance and slaves of vested interests." Santayana complained that James was beguiled by literary and theological illusions that caused him to misunderstand power and politics. Santayana mocked James' belief in the mythic American ideal as set forth in the Declaration of Independence. Indeed, Santayana pointed out that "the Declaration of Independence was a piece of literature, a salad of illusion" (ibid., 404).

Roosevelt's imperialistic idealism, Santayana's cynicism, and James' anti-imperialism together show us the tension within the American tradition. On the one hand, American politics is idealistically motivated by ideas about progress and civilization. On the other hand, power politics and war are always just below the surface. And at the other end of things, there is moralistic reluctance to affirm force as the engine of history. Throughout this tradition, there is ambivalence about war: on the one hand, war is horrible and undemocratic; on the other hand, war produces certain virtues and organizes people in powerful ways.

THE FIRST WORLD WAR

There are outright pacifists in the American tradition. But it is important to note that they are in the minority. Indeed, the most prominent pacifists are literally "minorities"—people at the margins—women and people of color like Addams, King, and Chavez; or members of minority religions such as the Amish, the Quakers, and the Mennonites. These outsiders have a very different vision of social justice than mainstream politicians such as Roosevelt or Woodrow Wilson. Wilson, for example, took the United States into the First World War with the idea that the war would be a war to end all wars.

> The world must be made safe for democracy. Its peace must be planted upon the tested foundations of political liberty. We have no selfish ends to serve. We desire no conquest, no dominion. We seek no indemnities for ourselves, no material compensation for the sacrifices we shall freely make. (Wilson, Speech to Congress, April 2, 1917)

It took an outsider such as Addams to note the contradiction in the Wilsonian idea. The United States entered the war in order to continue its efforts to become a global power; but it sold the war as a war for democracy. American business interests were so tied up with British interests, that some accused the United States of entering the war as a way of defending Wall Street. At any rate, there was no pressing need for the United States to enter the war in 1917. These sorts of contradictions were noted, at least by Jane Addams. Addams had believed that Wilson was a pacifist. She had met with him to discuss peaceful resolution of the European conflict in 1915. Addams worked directly for peace during the First World War, as President of the Women's International League for Peace and Freedom. In her speech at Carnegie Hall in 1915, Addams indicated the problem of the idea of using war to end war and establish democracy: "the longer the war goes on the more the military power is breaking down all the safeguards of civil life and of the civil government" (Addams, 2005b, 86). Addams had once believed that Wilson agreed with the peace camp. Indeed, she campaigned for Wilson's reelection in 1916, in which Wilson's campaign slogan was "he kept us out of the war." Addams was at a loss to explain why Wilson suddenly changed from pacifist to warmonger in the spring of 1917. Addams insisted in opposition to Wilson that the United States had a great opportunity to change the terms of the crisis by abjuring military power: "The crisis offered a test of the vigor and originality of a nation whose very foundations were laid upon a willingness to experiment" (Addams, 1922, 61).

The effort to reorient the war system obviously failed to take hold, in part because the pacifist movement was a minority movement at the margins. And media propaganda and political rhetoric inflamed war fever that led to anti-immigrant violence and massive violations of civil liberties used to keep dissenters in check. As Duane Cady concludes, "James' moral equivalent did not capture the imagination of the public. World War I did" (Cady, 1990, 139). To say that the First World War provoked conflict and consternation among American intellectuals is an understatement. Despite his sympathies for German culture, Josiah Royce condemned German submarine warfare and supported the war against Germany, even as he proposed an international insurance corporation as an antidote to war. Unlike Addams, Dewey supported Wilson's idealistic vision of a war to end war. Dewey's idealism was connected with a general hope for the progressive collective power that would be unleashed by the great national project of going to war. Dewey considered himself to be a sort of intelligent pacifist. But he was opposed to absolute pacifism, which he described as "squeamishness about force" that is the mark "not of idealistic but of moonstruck morals" (Dewey, 1983, 211).

One of Dewey's students, the pacifist Randolph Bourne, was sorely disappointed by Dewey's support of the War. Dewey thought that sometimes war can be a progressive force for social change. But Bourne claimed that Dewey was out of touch with reality and that he failed to understand the "heady and virulent poison of war" (Bourne, 1919, 117). Bourne claimed that the pragmatists of the Wilson era were too blind to see the toxicity of war. And he argued that Dewey had betrayed the spirit of William James. Bourne described war as antithetical to individuality and democracy and even to freedom of thought among the intellectual class: "Once the war is on, the conviction spreads that individual thought is helpless, that the only way one can count is as a cog in the great wheel" (Bourne, 1999, 12). While Dewey was hopeful about the great social project of the war, Bourne echoes Thoreau's idea about being a "counter-friction to the machine."

The difficulty of modern life is that we are both cogs in the machine and individuals who refuse to be ground down and used in this way. We are both committed to peace but stimulated by war. We benefit from great projects of social cooperation; but the greatest of these is war, which also brings destruction in its wake.

Supporters of the First World War focused on the ideals for which the war was being fought. Royce notes, for example, that democracies fight for noble democratic ideals. "Modern wars are in many cases deliberately and thoughtfully planned by patriots who love their country's honor, who are clearly conscious of well-formulated ideals which they think righteous, and who fight in the name of the freedom of the people, and in the service of what they suppose to be the highest human culture" (Royce, 1916, 6). Individuals do indeed volunteer to fight for wars of abolition or to spread civilization to the "men sitting in darkness" or to make the world safe for democracy. But the great paradox of war is that the individuals who volunteer are also used and abused by the central power for which they sacrifice themselves. And war rarely produces the sorts of goods its defenders hope for. This is the lesson of the senseless destruction of the First World War and its aftermath. This insight seems to have led Dewey to change his view of war. In 1939, Dewey concluded that "if there is one conclusion to which human experience unmistakably points, it is that democratic ends demand democratic methods for their realization" (Dewey, 1993a, 205). Of course, in 1939, an even more dangerous sort of militarism would emerge in Europe and Asia. And Americans would again move beyond pacifism and embrace war under the leadership of another member of the Roosevelt family.

FASCISM, TRANSCENDENTALISM, AND STOICISM

The fascists of the twentieth century extended the militaristic views of earlier thinkers in a more blatantly collectivist and racist direction. The philosophical background of fascism has been traced back to Nietzsche and Hegel. While we might debate any direct connection here, militarists and fascists tend to see war as a sublime and metaphysical necessity in the way explained by Hegel. The difference is that while Hegel described this fact, the fascists embraced and celebrated it. The Italian prefascist, Marinetti, put it this way in his "Futurist Manifesto": "We want to glorify war—the only cure for the world—militarism, patriotism, the destructive gesture of the anarchists, the beautiful ideas which kill, and contempt for woman."

American philosophers explicitly rejected both the quasi-religious view of war and the biological reductionism of those like Nietzsche and the social Darwinists who claim that war is a way of culling the herd. Addams and James both maintained that—as James put it: "apologists for war at the present day take it religiously" (James, 1987, 1284; Addams, 1911, chapter 8). James quotes the German sociologist Rudolf Steinmetz as claiming that war "is an ordeal instituted by God, who weighs the nations in its balance" (James, 1987, 1286). The problem with this point of view is that it makes the grinding scourge of war into a metaphysical necessity, while romanticizing the state, patriotism, and martial virtues. The American philosophical tradition has little tolerance for this collectivizing idealism. Even an American idealist like Royce explicitly rejects Steinmetz's philosophy of war. Royce claims that he adopted the title of his book *The Philosophy of Loyalty* from Steinmetz' book, *The Philosophy of War*. But according to Royce, Steinmetz is wrong that war is the best way to develop key virtues such as patriotism and loyalty.

America's philosophers are generally opposed to a metaphysical celebration of war and the state, just as they are generally opposed to biological reductionism and racial views of history and culture. Thus, pragmatists opposed Imperialism and the ideology of the white man's burden. The Anti-Imperialist League had affirmed, for example, in 1898 that "all men, of whatever race or color, are entitled to life, liberty and the pursuit of happiness." Racism and collectivism of the sort that is typical of fascism does not fit well with the American emphasis on individuality. And thus by the Second World War, especially after the attacks of Pearl Harbor, the mainstream consensus was in favor of a war against the perversity of fascism. Although Dewey was originally opposed to American intervention—as a result of a less optimistic view of war that developed after the senseless suffering of the First World War—Dewey did mount an attack on the Nazi *Weltanschauung*. Dewey dissected

Hitler's ideology and condemned it for its anti-individualism, its racial ideals, and its valorization of force, cruelty, and hatred (Dewey, 2008). Indeed, Dewey went so far as to argue that Hitler's views were a profane corruption of the German philosophical tradition, which Dewey traced back to Kant, Fichte, and Hegel.

It seems obvious that American philosophers would be opposed to fascist and Nazi ideology. Philosophers in the American tradition focus on liberty, intelligent action, hope for the future, and respect for individuality. These ideas form what might be called "American Stoicism" (see Lachs, 2005 and Furtak, 2003). But the very idea of combining pragmatism and Stoicism indicates a source of ambivalence and conflict: the Stoic desire for equanimity and tranquility combine uneasily with the pragmatic interest in changing the world for the better. Lachs claims that pragmatism and stoicism are moods—each of which are useful in different contexts: pragmatism is the active and melioristic mood; stoicism is the passive and contemplative mood. Like Greek and Roman Stoicism, American Stoicism is dedicated to the idea that philosophical reflection and the philosophical virtues are essential to a life well lived. But unlike ancient Stoicism, American Stoicism is shaped by modern liberal values, such as the idea that each individual has equal worth and that intelligent human action can help to create a better world. Unlike ancient Stoicism, American philosophers disavow faith in providence and a hierarchical view of social life, even while they affirm the power of collective social action. This view results in an uncomfortable compromise with state power. The philosophers in the American tradition are not libertarians or anarchists—despite the fact that they emphasize individual liberty. They recognize that state action—and perhaps even war—can be beneficial, even while they criticize militarism. The tension here is between a view that values individual liberty and one that recognizes the power of the collective.

The American tradition prides itself on a sort of Stoic resolve in the face of adversity. Americans have long celebrated the courage that it takes to confront life's daily tasks. This courageous, "can-do" attitude is especially important in times of adversity—especially in wartime. Franklin Delano Roosevelt is well known for the phrase, "there is nothing to fear but fear itself." Roosevelt initially offered this aphorism as a response to the Great Depression; but it resonated with the war against fascism. This claim can be traced back through the virile virtues of FDR's cousin, Theodore Roosevelt, and on back to Thoreau who had written in a journal entry (September 7, 1851), "Nothing is so much to be feared as fear" (Thoreau, 1906, vol. 7, 468). These words are quoted with approval by Emerson in his essay on Thoreau (Emerson, 2000, 825). Emerson himself wrote that "fear disenchants life and the world" (Emerson, 1929, vol. 2, 973).

In this way, the Stoic resolve and self-reliant individualism of American Transcendentalism came to inspire American idealism in the Second World War. But this war also reminds us, once again, of the deep ambiguity of war. American forces fought in defense of liberty and human rights. But the United States succumbed to racial profiling in the internment of Japanese Americans. And the United States is the first and only military power on earth to utilize atomic weapons in warfare—the most indiscriminate and collective killer ever devised.

CONCLUSION

We've seen deep ambivalence in the American tradition. On the one hand, war promotes certain noble virtues, while inspiring collective action that can be aimed at creating progress in history. On the other hand, war is destructive and undemocratic. War does treat individuals as cogs in the machine, even when that machine is oriented toward some progressive social good. These tensions are unavoidable. They reflect our conflicting moods and the tragic conflicts that we find in social and political life. It is no wonder, then that on the very day that the Japanese attacked Pearl Harbor, Dewey found himself overwhelmed and inarticulate, with nothing to say about the war (see Diggins, 1994). The horrible brutality of war shows us a failure of reason and of speech. And at times like those, the wise response may well be to revert to the Stoic mood with courage and hope—but also with a recognition of the dangers and disastrous implications of war.

CHAPTER NINE

SLIDING SCALES AND THE MISCHIEF OF WAR

War is mischief upon the largest scale.

Jeremy Bentham, "Of War"

Our moral intuitions are fragile and inconsistent. War magnifies value conflicts in the largest way imaginable, producing mischief on the largest scale. The basic conflict in moral theory—between deontological ethics and utilitarianism—becomes obvious and acute in war. As the most extreme of all human activities, war reminds us that it is impossible to remain consistently good.

The best attempt we have at making sense of the moral conflicts we find in war is the just war theory. The just war theory incorporates both utilitarian and deontological concerns and coordinates these conflicting values on a sliding scale. But this hybrid approach provides an unsatisfying compromise. Attempts to explain and rationalize compromises by way of a sliding scale are unsatisfying for advocates of moral purity of either the utilitarian or deontological varieties. Absolute pacifism is usually deontological: it maintains that our duty is to avoid violence; and any compromise with war is a violation of that duty. However, realism is usually utilitarian: it seeks to maximize benefits and efficiency. From this perspective, limits on warfare get in the way of quick victory that would end war and return us to peace. The just war theory represents a compromise that will not be satisfying either to pacifists, deontologists, realists, or utilitarians. There is simply no way to come up with a final and consistent moral response to war that does not sacrifice serious goods.

These conflicts are revealed when we consider "back-to-the-wall" scenarios and "supreme emergencies," such as what to do with a terrorist who has a ticking bomb or how to respond to nuclear threats. In such situations, even ardent pacifists may be willing to flirt with violence. And when whole civilizations are under threat of annihilation, it becomes easy to consider massive and indiscriminate violence such as that imagined by the MADness of nuclear deterrent strategy. As J.L. Mackie once put it, "The most plausible absolute prohibitions must be violated where strict adherence to them would result in disaster" (Mackie, 1977, 168). We should be careful not to base our conclusions about life and morality upon generalizations derived from the contemplation of imagined disasters. Hard cases make bad law, as the saying goes. But disaster scenarios and supreme emergencies do help us see basic conflicts of values.

One way of dealing with disaster scenarios is to conceive of moral judgment on a sliding scale in which deontological concerns gradually give way to concern for consequences and the greater good. Sliding scales are linked to what are called, following W.D. Ross, prima facie or pro tanto duties—duties that are taken as rules of thumb or generalizations that are not absolute. Prima facie duties can be overridden by other duties and values.

The idea of a sliding scale has been discussed by several important thinkers who write about terrorism and war. Michael Walzer, for example, speaks of the sliding scale as providing us with guidance during moments of catastrophe or supreme emergency. On Walzer's interpretation, the sliding scale is set up with a certain amount of friction that tends to resist violating principles of the war convention. At some point, "the convention is overridden, but only in the face of an imminent catastrophe" (Walzer, 1977, 232). When disaster is imminent it becomes permissible to set deontological prohibitions aside and use torture, terror bombing, or other sorts of violence that appear to violate the war convention. One can rig the sliding scale in various ways, depending upon the weight given to the parameters involved. While the sliding scale idea is a useful heuristic, it does not provide a final solution. Rather, the resort to the sliding scale is an indication of value conflict.

DEONTOLOGICAL AND UTILITARIAN VIEWS OF PUNISHMENT

At one end of such a sliding scale, is the ideal of nonmaleficence and respect for persons. The idea of *primum non nocere*, "first, do no harm," fits with the idea of not using persons as a means for other ends. At the other end of the sliding scale is utilitarian concern for "greatest happiness for the greatest number," which admits that in some circumstances, some persons may be harmed to benefit the greater number. For the utilitarian, it might be necessary to use some persons in order to produce the greatest happiness for the greatest number. We can see these conflicting values in the different ideas about punishment that are defended by Kant and Bentham. These discussions of punishment provide a microcosm in which to consider deontological and utilitarian approaches to the justification of political violence.

The basic Kantian principle of respect for the dignity of persons creates an obligation not to harm innocent persons, even if harming them might help others—say in the case where punishing a terrorist's wife or daughter might lead a terrorist to defuse his bomb. Moreover, on Kant's view, respect for persons explains why we punish wrongdoers. If a person has done wrong, then they deserve to be punished. Punishment expresses respect for the wrongdoer by giving him what he deserves. Kant defends the death penalty as a fitting punishment for murder because "undeserved evil which any one commits on another, is to be regarded as perpetrated on himself" (Kant, 1887, Part II, Section 49.E). According to Kant's idea of the Categorical Imperative, maxims of actions ought to be universalized. When the maxim of murder is universalized, the murderer is in effect saying that he should be murdered. Out of respect for the murderer, then we should give him what he has intended.

Kant goes so far as to maintain that it would be wrong not to execute murderers. Kant explains that if a society were to disband and its prisons were to close, the murderers awaiting execution must be killed before we could close the prison. While Kant thought that the guilty deserve to be punished, he also maintains that the innocent deserve to be left unmolested. Moreover, Kant also recognizes that in punishing the guilty, there are deontological limits. Despite the fact that they may be killed, murderers may not be tortured. As Kant puts it, the murderer's death "must be kept free from all maltreatment that would make the humanity suffering in his person loathsome or abominable" (Kant, 1887, Part II, Section 49.E). Even when executing justice, it is necessary to respect the dignity of persons and to avoid circumstances that degrade humanity or use persons as a means to some further end.

At the other end of the conflict of values, utilitarians will argue that it may be necessary to use persons as examples to send a message that aims at promoting the greater good. The basic idea of deterrence is to threaten violence in order to prevent violence. This strategy of threat is crucial for nuclear deterrent strategy, where the threat of killing massive numbers of civilians worked to prevent nuclear war between the Soviets and Americans during the Cold War. In the domestic case, the system of punishment uses the convicted criminal as an example, harming him to deter others. Similarly, torture—both interrogative and terroristic—can be justified by utilitarianism. Interrogative torture can be justified if the information discovered through torture will save lives or benefit others. Terroristic torture can be used to send a message aimed at producing some greater good—for example, compliance with the law. The utilitarian philosopher Jeremy Bentham chronicled a variety of tortures and punishments in his *Rationale of Punishment*: from tattooing, branding, and flaying the nostrils to whipping, amputations, and other forms of corporal punishment.

A key concern for Bentham is the question of whether corporal punishments actually work to reduce crime. Unlike Kant who states that we must give people what they deserve regardless of the consequences, utilitarians like Bentham are interested in empirical research into results and consequences. For many of the punishments he considers, Bentham indicates that it is an open question as to whether they work. One of the problems for Bentham is that since punishments are applied inconsistently, it is difficult to know whether they work. To remedy this problem, Bentham proposes a whipping or caning machine that would administer corporal punishment en masse. This would standardize the punishment, while also increasing the terror that it produced. The hope is that this standardized and terrifying punishment would prevent crime. At the same time, Bentham is not a supporter of the death penalty. He is not convinced it works to prevent crime. He is worried that it tends to be abused by tyrannical governments. And he argues that if convicted murderers were given a punishment of life in prison spent at hard labor, this may produce more social good than execution would—since prison labor can be used for social benefit.

This brief discussion of Kant's and Bentham's views of punishment shows us the conflict between utilitarians and deontologists. Kant thinks that murderers deserve to die but should not be tortured. Bentham believes that we should not execute murderers if their labor can be put to use, but he holds that torture may produce good results.

This sort of conflict can be discerned in the heart of the just war tradition. On the one hand, deontological principles demand that war should only be undertaken when there is a just cause. One obvious just cause is to punish aggressive nations for the crime of aggression. There may be a related duty to go to war to defend people against genocide or domestic oppression. We might say that humanitarian interventions are morally required to defend the innocent and to give evil dictators what they deserve. In this sense, just cause can be linked to the idea of respect for human beings: we respect human beings by defending them when they are innocent and punishing them when they are guilty. But deontological principles limit what can be done in war. According to principles of *jus in bello*, civilians cannot be deliberately targeted; rape and torture cannot be employed as weapons of war; and surrendering soldiers must be taken prisoner and treated well.

On the other hand, utilitarian interpretations of just cause would focus on the question of whether war produces more good than harm. We see this in the just war principle of "proportionality": the benefit of the war is supposed to outweigh the harms caused. Moreover, war is supposed to be a reasonable last resort: meaning we should try other nonviolent means to produce our desired result before we take up arms. Judgments about proportionality and last resort should be grounded in empirical data about what works. These sorts of judgments may vary depending on context—unlike the deontological judgment, which is a priori and which thus ignores context. Since the concern is whether war will produce the desired benefit, utilitarians will also be willing to make exceptions to the deontological prohibitions of *jus in bello*. In a supreme emergency, utilitarian concerns may trump deontological principles as the goal of victory (or self-preservation) overrides any other concern. At that point, torture, terror bombing, and killing prisoners becomes a possibility.

It is important to note that Kant and Bentham were both generally opposed to war. In the 1780s and 1790s, Kant and Bentham each devised a plan aimed at peace. But moralistic opposition to war runs aground on the reality that wars occur despite their great mischief. And so Bentham and Kant each offer a compromise with war.

Kant is opposed to war because it tends to use persons as means: warfare ends up harming the innocent. Kant says, "the establishment of a universal and enduring peace is not just a part, but rather constitutes the whole of the ultimate purpose of justice and law within the bounds of pure reason" (Kant, 1965b, 163). Kant thus concludes that the norm of peace is derived a priori: it is a principle of reason and not the result of empirical research. Nonetheless, Kant recognized that since war was not going to be eradicated any time soon, it was necessary to limit war by principles of justice in war. And this is why Kant outlined preliminary articles of peace in his essay *Perpetual Peace*. These rules are only necessary in a world in which we have to accommodate ourselves to the mischief of war. But if there must be war, there are some things that should not be done: no assassinations, no poisoning, etc.

For utilitarians, there is no a priori reason to be opposed to war— since utilitarians reject a priori reasoning as a guide for morality. While Bentham was generally opposed to war, he did recognize that war could be necessary for the greater good. But even within war, Bentham held that there were practical utilitarian limits. In order to reduce cruelty, war should be waged against its intended target—the government and military—and not against the people. Moreover, Bentham maintained that the scorched earth approach to warfare was ineffective, since inhumane armies provoke passionate opposition. Bentham indicates that violations of *jus in bello* are generally ineffective. But it could turn out that they work—there is no a priori certainty here.

TORTURE, WAR, AND THE DOCTRINE OF DOUBLE EFFECT

These conflicting values show up in recent discussions of war and torture in the United States. There is great squeamishness about torture, as indicated by the outrage over Abu Ghraib and the ongoing discussions by the Justice Department, the Pentagon, and the Senate about practices such as waterboarding. The international community appears to agree that torture is wrong and official U.S. policy disavows torture, even while admitting that the CIA has, for example, used waterboarding during the war on terrorism. What is odd here is that we should be so squeamish about torture while wars rage in Afghanistan and Iraq. In terms of suffering and desert, the torture of terrorist masterminds such as Khalid Sheikh

Mohammed seems a trivial concern compared to the killing of innocent children that has occurred in Iraq and Afghanistan. The children killed in these conflicts did nothing to deserve to be killed, while KSM, as he is called, was actively involved in Al-Qaeda. And the psychological and physiological harm done to KSM is minor in comparison to the deaths of these innocent bystanders. It would seem that if we can justify war, then we should easily justify the targeted violence of interrogative torture.

One might argue that it would be even more effective to torture members of KSM's family. While a terror-bomber's family is presumably innocent, torture that targets innocent members of the terrorist's family would at least be more likely to have a positive result than the sort of widespread destruction of innocent life that occurs in war. But oddly enough many people believe that the deaths of the innocent in war can be justified, while the suffering that is inflicted on a terrorist during torture cannot. And most would seem to agree with Fritz Allhoff that raping a terrorist's daughter or burning his mother are simply wrong and should not be done, no matter whether it works or not (Allhoff, 2003). Basically, we believe it would be wrong to use an individual purely as a means to some other end: and raping the terrorist's daughter would be exactly such a violation.

However, the same sort of argument can be made against war: the individuals who are killed in warfare as collateral damage are used in a very similar way. We must admit that there are differences here in terms of intention: the torturer directly intends the harm caused, while a just warrior unintentionally kills the innocent. The doctrine of double effect can be employed to justify unintentional killing. But the doctrine of double effect only works within an ethical framework that takes intentions seriously. Consequentialists are less interested in the vagaries of intention and more interested in results. And if results alone matter, then there is no good reason not to torture a terrorist or rape his daughter—so long as these actions produce the desired outcome.

Some have explicitly argued that torture can be worse than killing in war. Henry Shue, for example, claims that war is like a fair fight in which soldiers have a more or less equal chance of killing or being killed. Shue goes on to claim that torture is unfair because the one who is tortured is defenseless. Despite this Shue imagines some criteria for justifying torture: it should be used rarely and only for supremely important moral goods; and torture would have to be the least harmful means of attaining these goods. With these criteria in mind, Shue articulates a *reductio ad absurdum* of torture: the conditions for acceptable torture are so stringent that torture cannot be justified in the real world in which torturers are not saints with perfect self-control (Shue, 1978, 139).

Shue acknowledges that empirical and historical details must be used to support this claim: it rests upon a claim about the likelihood that torture would be misused and excessive. Given a wealth of historical precedents—including recent events at Bagram Air Force base in Afghanistan, at Abu Ghraib in Iraq, and at Guantamo in Cuba—we should be reluctant to affirm the use of torture. One of the important features of these recent examples is that innocent persons were caught and tortured (see Hegland, 2006). There are also serious doubts about whether torture is effective in the long run. But for a utilitarian, the question of innocence is not decisive; and it may turn out that torture is effective in some cases. Thus, a utilitarian will be more open to torture—even torturing a terror-bomber's wife or daughter.

While I agree with Shue's basic conclusions regarding the difficulty of justifying torture, I believe that the same sort of reasoning applies to war. The just war tradition gives us a set of criteria for the restraint of war. But in reality, no war lives up to these criteria. It is quite odd, then, that Shue and others think that torture is more difficult to justify than warfare. It would seem that the reverse is true. In general, the reason for this seemingly confusing conclusion is the deontological doctrine of double effect. The doctrine of double effect tells us to look at the intentions of an action and not at the results. If the intentions are good, then inadvertent harms can be permitted—even when they are massive harms such as occur in war. At the same time, deontological ethics would prohibit actions that intend deliberate harm to the innocent or to the defenseless, as in the case of torture. Utilitarians are, of course, not so interested in intentions—and so they would reject the doctrine of double effect.

One need not be a Kantian to criticize torture on deontological grounds. Consider Derek Jeffrey's critique of torture: Jeffreys grounds his critique of torture in personalist philosophers who emphasize the importance of empathy (Jeffreys, 2006). According to Jeffreys, torture is wrong because it dehumanizes its victims (and its perpetrators) by a process that eliminates empathy. Jeffreys holds that empathy is the capacity through which we connect with the inner life of other persons, in what Jeffreys calls "solidarity." According to Jeffreys, proper empathy should prevent us from torturing other human beings, since when we identify with others, we understand both their experience of suffering and the fact that all persons have dignity that deserves respect. This line of reasoning echoes deontological themes while developing a point made by Shue: torture is wrong because it is an act that intentionally inflicts harm upon a defenseless person. It is the defenselessness of the victim that is the key here: it makes sense to fight to defend myself against a person who is attacking me; but when that person has been subdued and no longer poses a threat, it is no longer morally justifiable to inflict harm on him.

The idea here is that violence must be minimized and when it is not absolutely necessary to harm a person, we should not intentionally do harm. It might seem that on this view, the death penalty would be practically abolished, as Pope John Paul II has argued in *Evangelium Vitae*. Deontological ethicists might respond by claiming that this sort of softness toward murderers fails to give the murderers what they deserve. Others, such as Jeffrey Reiman (1985) and J.L.A. Garcia (2003), argue that there may be good reasons to give people less than what they deserve in terms of the *lex talionis*. The key in all these discussions is intention. To intend to harm a defenseless human being is wrong. But with torture (whether interrogative or terroristic), the intention is to use the torture victim as a means. Kant would claim that this is disrespectful. Jeffreys would argue that it destroys empathy and solidarity. And thus, torture is wrong from the deontological standpoint—even if it works.

One would think that this deontological approach would also lead to a prohibition against war. War kills innocent human beings in a way that appears disrespectful. But the doctrine of double effect is used by deontological ethicists to allow the killing of innocents in war so long as it is not intentional. But there is an odd tension here. If we take empathy so seriously—as Jeffreys does—that we are unwilling to allow torture, then war must also be wrong, since empathy would seem to link us to the suffering of the innocent victims of war. But the deontological response would again appeal to double effect: even if we empathize with innocents killed in war, their deaths are permitted provided they are not directly intended.

Perhaps Shue, Jeffreys, or other critics of torture who defend war imagine a very limited and sanitized version of military force—surgical strikes against known targets. But this kind of precision is rare: surgical strikes go awry, intelligence can be faulty, and innocents are very easily harmed. If we could ensure that no (or very few) innocents would be harmed, or that the harm would be minor, then we may be able to justify these activities. But the fog of war prevents this sort of certainty and experience tells us that war puts innocents at serious risk of loss of life.

Some bite the bullet and admit that anything goes in war. Indeed utilitarians will argue that if the goal is to win and get on with the peace—and to do so quickly in order to minimize the mischief of war—then we should not be squeamish about the means employed. Others employ the just war theory but end up with similar conclusions. Andrew Valls considered the link between terrorism and war in a recent article and concluded, "if war can be justified, then terrorism can be as well" (Valls, 2006, 326). Now absolute pacifists will condemn all state sponsored killing because they hold that all killing is wrong. But Valls' point is more subtle: that the just war theory is permissive enough to allow attacks that we would consider to be terrorism—attacks that knowingly kill the innocent. Others, like Michael Walzer, will argue that the just war theory precludes terrorism by definition, since the just war theory will not permit deliberately targeting the innocent. And yet, Walzer does allow for terror bombing to be employed in extreme "back-to-the-wall" circumstances according to what he calls "the supreme emergency" exemption. This appears to be a contradiction. One way around this is to employ the doctrine of double effect as described above. Another way around this conclusion is to hold that moral principles are not absolute; but rather that they are prima facie values adjustable on the sliding scale.

PLURAL SLIDING SCALES

The justification of violence involves a number of considerations. Among the most important are: *who* is harmed, *how much* they are harmed, and *how certain* we are that they will be harmed. These considerations can be tied together in a judgment that compares harms and benefits by way of a sliding scale with three variables.

Unfortunately, the problem is that there are various ways to explain the sliding scale and its structure of prima facie duties.

Here are two versions of such a sliding scale. First, consider a sliding scale that puts nonmaleficence as the primary value. We can call this the deontological sliding scale.

The Deontological Sliding Scale: The *prima facie* duty of *primum non nocere* can only be overridden for obvious and important benefits. The benefits of an activity that may harm innocent persons must be weighed against the likelihood, the seriousness, and the extensiveness of the harm. In general, the more likely, the more serious, and the more extensive the harm, the more difficult it is to justify that activity, unless the purported benefits are more certain, more serious, and more extensive.

The presumption behind this sliding scale is that activities that involve harm to innocent persons are, *prima facie*, not justifiable. The assumption that the primary obligation of political action is *primum non nocere*—to do no harm—fits well within the standard way of conceiving political action among those who take the idea of rights seriously. Rights are defenses against harm. Although the state may want to undertake activities that promote the greater good, the idea of rights as defenses from harm, will impose a serious limit on such activities. From this perspective, the burden of proof rests upon the proponent of an activity that will harm innocents since, by definition, the innocent have done nothing to deserve to be harmed. This burden requires that the proponent consider the three variables mentioned in proportion to the purported benefit: the likelihood of harm (how certain are we?), the seriousness of harm (how much harm?), and the extent of the harm (who will be harmed?). The first variable is epistemic, the second is physiological and psychological, and the third is social. Although the parameters involved here do reflect some of the concerns of Bentham's hedonic calculus (certainty and extent, for example), this sliding scale is not utilitarian, since it is not concerned with *maximizing* the greatest happiness for the greatest number. Rather, it is concerned with *minimizing* harm to the innocent. This sliding scale does not establish an absolute prohibition against war or torture; however, it makes it very difficult to justify war.

Unfortunately, utilitarians will not easily agree to this version of the sliding scale, since it is possible to recalibrate the scale in a way that downplays individual rights and nonmaleficence. Consider this version of a utilitarian sliding scale.

The Utilitarian Sliding Scale: The *prima facie* duty of *maximizing the greatest happiness for the greatest number* can only be overridden when there are risks of massive and widespread harms to persons. An activity that has obvious and widespread potential benefits should only be prohibited if it is likely that there will be serious and extensive harm. In general, the more likely, the more felicific, and the more extensive the benefit, the more difficult it is to prohibit that activity, unless the purported benefits are far outweighed by more certain, more serious, and more extensive harms.

This way of putting things assumes that the primary goal is to maximize public welfare and the greater good. This sort of sliding scale helps to explain, for example, Mill's ideas about foreign interventions. Mill assumed that the spread of civilization was such an important benefit that warfare could be justified in order to bring about the spread of civilization—even if this meant paternalistic despotism for barbarians. At the same time, Mill recognized that within European powers, where the good of "civilization" was already in place, the mischief of war among civilized nations far outweighed any purported benefit.

With the utilitarian sliding scale, the burden of proof is altered, even though we can use the same three sorts of questions discussed with regard to the deontological sliding scale: epistemic, psychological/physiological, and social. Here the burden requires that an opponent of war show the likelihood of harm (how certain are we?), the seriousness of harm (how much harm?), and the extent of the harm (who will be harmed?). Standards of proof here will be based upon background assumptions about war and its efficacy for promoting utilitarian happiness.

While we might think that a sliding scale approach can help solve the conflict of values we've been discussing, it turns out that these sliding scales merely reiterate the problem. The idea of using a sliding scale to resolve conflicting values in the justification (or rejection) of war cannot resolve the conflict of values because there are a variety of ways of constructing the sliding scale. We've discussed two such scales. But other versions could be constructed.

This basic fact is overlooked by proponents and defenders of the just war theory who believe that the just war theory and the idea of the sliding scale provide an easy mechanism for think-ing about the justification of war. With Walzer, the idea is that the more just the cause and the more supreme the emergency, the more violence can be used in its pursuit. In the *Law of Peoples*, Rawls explicitly affirms Walzer's idea and its implications for the idea of a supreme emergency exception to principles of justice in war. And, interestingly enough, in another context Rawls applies the sliding scale concept to conscientious objection: the more the cause is unjust, the more justified one is in objecting (Rawls, 1971, 381). Henry Shue has further clarified Walzer's idea by noting the difference between a *limited* sliding scale and an *unlimited* one (Shue, 2004, chapter 7). A limited sliding scale would still hold some actions as always morally wrong, while an unlimited sliding scale would be willing to allow almost any amount of violence if the cause were momentous enough. In different language, a lim-ited sliding scale would hold certain deontological principles as absolute constraints, while an unlimited sliding scale would be an entirely consequentialist scale that ignored such side constraints in pursuit of the greater good.

Utilitarian and deontological principles appear to give us incom-mensurable conclusions about emergencies. Absolute deontolo-gists will argue that no human person should ever be used merely as a means—even to prevent massive casualties. Utilitarians will see things otherwise, defending even deliberate harm done to some individuals from the standpoint of the greater good. Even moderate deontologists and utilitarians who are willing to compromise will construct different versions of the sliding scale that fit with their own views about moral theory.

THRESHOLD DEONTOLOGY AND VALUE PLURALISM

The sliding scale idea can be supplemented by considerations of so-called threshold deontology. Similar to Shue's idea of a limited sliding scale, this approach keeps deontological principles as nearly absolute. It only allows a switch to utilitarian concerns once a cer-tain threshold of harm is crossed. Threshold deontologists would reject torture or terror tactics in war unless some key threshold of harm were reached. The problem for threshold deontology is where and how to draw the line that creates the threshold. At bottom here is the question of when (and why) the numbers begin to count.

Drawing on the work of John Taurek, Larry Alexander has argued against threshold deontology such as he finds in the work of Michael Moore, Thomas Nagel, and Robert Nozick (Alexander, 2000). Alexander indicates that one way of conceiving the switch from deontological prohibitions to consequentialism is to imagine a dam overflowing. Once a certain threshold is reached—say when 1,000 people are threatened by a terror-bomber—then deontological prohibitions are overridden and utilitarian concern kicks in, just as water is continually added to a reservoir until finally the dam overflows. Once the threshold is reached, then we should choose to torture one in order to save 1,000 people. And in this sort of case, it doesn't matter whether we torture an innocent or a guilty party, so long as the torture works. In this way, we might justify torturing a terror-bomber's daughter, as a way of preventing massive harm that is above a certain threshold.

Alexander has exposed the problems of threshold deontology. One problem is that the threshold point is arbitrary: why is it permissible to torture a terror-bomber or his daughter when 1,000 potential victims may be harmed but not permissible when only 2 or 10 or 999 victims may be harmed? A related problem is that prior to reaching the threshold, those who may be killed by the terror-bomber are treated as so much "moral ballast" filling up the area behind the dam, until finally the threshold is reached. But the more fundamental problem is that if deontological prohibitions are taken seriously, they are always incommensurable with consequentialist justifications of harm. Alexander is right that those who are seriously committed to absolutist versions of deontological prohibitions can never be persuaded that at some point the numbers do count.

Threshold deontology and sliding scales admit that there are plural values in conflict. The difficulty is when and how to resolve the conflict. These approaches are based upon a pluralistic conception of prima facie values, which admits that there are a variety of plausible and defensible goods that can on occasion conflict. One principle is that we should not harm innocents without proper justification. Another principle is that we should take actions for the greater good. In the case of torturing the terror-bomber's daughter, these values conflict. The challenge is to find a general rubric that allows us to coordinate the plurality of goods. Unfortunately, there is no final solution to this challenge, as the discussion of whether "the numbers count" indicates. It is difficult to explain why the harm of 999 people does not exceed the threshold, while 1,001 does. And in this sense, a sliding scale might appear to make more sense than threshold deontology. Instead of treating each number up to the threshold as "moral ballast," the sliding scale continually adds up the numbers.

CONCLUSION

Whether we focus on threshold deontology or on a sliding scale, we must concede that there is no perfect compromise available. Sliding scales and thresholds are heuristic devices that help us coordinate conflicting values. But these heuristics cannot solve the problem of conflicting values. Our values are plural. Some people think that public utility is primary. Others are absolute pacifists. Even among those who agree that we need a sliding scale, there are disagreements. Some will believe that preventing harm to dozens is sufficient for us to use torture and terror bombing, while others will hold back and set the number much higher. There is no solution that is not based on some arbitrary stipulation or question-begging first principle. And this is why there is war in the first place. Plurality of values and arbitrariness are exactly what lead us to war.

The difficulty of the sliding scale and threshold deontology is that these ideas are subject to various interpretations, given the basic intuitions with which we begin. We see this problem in the just war tradition itself, which gives us several conflicting criteria for justifying violence. The just war tradition tends to allow harm to the innocent by way of the doctrine of double effect. This principle can be quite permissive, since its primary purpose is *not* to reduce harm. Indeed, for double effect, the numbers don't count. Thus, we can use double effect to justify widespread destruction—so long as the intention is legitimate. But at the same time, we cannot use double effect to justify torturing a terror-bomber's daughter, even though this may be more effective than widespread bombing at stopping a terrorist.

However, for utilitarians, torture and terror bombing can be justified if it produces the greatest happiness for the greatest number. The just war theory uses the term proportionality to describe this idea. Consider again the idea of torturing a terrorist's daughter. According to utilitarianism, if this were more effective than widespread bombing at preventing terrorism, then this is what we should do. It is better to torture one to produce a social benefit than to kill many to produce the same benefit. On this view, the numbers matter and if we can minimize harm while maximizing benefit, then that is what we should do, even if this destroys empathy or uses persons as a means.

And so we see, there are unavoidable conflicts in thinking about the justification of violence. There is no happy synthesis. Rather, this chapter should remind us of the ubiquity of conflict, the mischief of war, and the difficulty of moral judgment.

CHAPTER TEN

WATERBOARDING, TORTURE, AND VIOLENCE

*No moral value held dear by the American people obliges public
servants ever to sacrifice innocent lives to spare a captured terrorist
from unpleasant things.*

Dick Cheney, May 21, 2009

Torture is one of the most obvious places to look to see the conflict
between the utilitarian concerns of public life and the more deontological concerns of private ethics. In the previous chapter, I discussed the conflict between utilitarianism and deontology in terms
of a sliding scale. In the present chapter, I consider the complicated
question of defining and justifying torture. We seem to know what
torture is by ostensive definition. Most of us have a couple of paradigm images in mind of acts that can be called torture: flogging or
breaking on the rack. But problems occur at the edges of such lists,
as we've seen in the recent discussion of waterboarding. Some lists
of tortures are quite expansive. Some appear to think that almost
any form of violence is also a form of torture. In its discussion of
violence against women, the World Organization Against Torture
(OMCT) states:

> . . . the following acts are considered "torture": rape and sexual
> abuse, genital mutilation, incest, forced abortion, honor killings,
> dowry-related violence, forced marriages, human trafficking
> and forced prostitution.[1]

And then there are those, like Dick Cheney, who deny that waterboarding is torture, while also defending its use as an "enhanced
interrogation" method.

The debate about waterboarding is a fascinating example of moral conflict. The story can be traced back to Attorney General John Ashcroft, the President's Counsel (and later Attorney General) Alberto Gonzales, and the infamous "torture memos" of 2002. In a memo of August 1, 2002, the Assistant Attorney General, Jay Bybee defined torture as an act that inflicts pain that is "equivalent in intensity to the pain accompanying serious physical injury, such as organ failure, impairment of bodily function, or even death."[2] In reaction to this restrictive definition and its permissive stance regarding interrogation techniques, Congress attempted to legislate a broader and less permissive idea of torture in the Detainee Treatment Act (DTA) of 2005, a law that included the McCain Amendment and the Graham-Levin Amendment on Detainees. President Bush signed the DTA into law on December 30, 2005. Although this law was intended to restrict interrogative techniques and align CIA practices with the Army Field Manual, there is an ongoing debate about whether certain techniques—such as waterboarding—are ruled out. And this debate hinges on the question of whether waterboarding, in which water is dumped over a victim's face to simulate drowning, is really torture.

President Bush routinely said that the United States does not use torture, while hedging about whether waterboarding should be allowed. Waterboarding would not qualify as torture under the permissive definition given in Bybee's memo, quoted above. In early February 2007, CIA Director Michael Hayden admitted in congressional testimony that the United States has used waterboarding in the war on terrorism, employing the technique on detainees such as Khalid Sheik Mohammed, although Hayden also claimed that the technique has not been used since the passage of the DTA and a subsequent Supreme Court decision. The Bush White House continued to claim that waterboarding can be used in case of an emergency. Although waterboarding is no longer being employed, we are just beginning to learn about the details of its use in conjunction with other "enhanced interrogation techniques" in the war on terrorism. It turns out that Khalid Sheik Mohammed and others were waterboarded repeatedly. According to the *New York Times* (April 19, 2009), the CIA admitted that waterboarding was used on Khalid Sheik Mohammed 183 times. And waterboarding was employed in conjunction with a variety of other abuses. These prisoners were kept disoriented, naked, and cold. They were slammed against walls, given suppositories, prevented from sleeping, and kept in stress positions. The Red Cross concluded:

> The allegations of ill-treatment of the detainees indicate that, in many cases, the ill-treatment to which they were subjected while held in the CIA program, either singly or in combination, constituted torture. In addition, many other elements of the ill-treatment, either singly or in combination, constituted cruel, inhuman or degrading treatment. (Quoted in Danner, 2009)

NORMATIVE DEFINITIONS OF TORTURE

It is obvious that practices such as waterboarding are in need of careful moral scrutiny. The practice intends to coerce its victims by producing fear, panic, and pain. This is true whether we call the practice "torture" or not. Political rhetoric and confusion about terminology should not distract us from commonsense wisdom that holds that actions, such as waterboarding, that cause harm require moral justification. And in the same way, forced prostitution and the other acts identified as torture by OMCT are wrong—whether we call them torture or some other name. The more harmful the practice the more difficult it is to justify it, whether we call it torture or not.

Any definition of torture will have to admit that torture is an activity that deliberately inflicts harm on a person against their will. It uses a person's physiological responses—fear, pain, etc.—against that person in order to coerce the person into compliance. The etymology of "torture" shows us this. The term can be traced back to the idea of twisting or changing shape—as in a torturous road or in the idea of distortion or contortion. The Latin ancestor is *torquere*, which has a cognate in the English word "torque" or twisting force. Torture twists the individual, distorts his body and mind, and turns him against himself: the person's physiological and psychological responses are twisted and turned upon the person such that he betrays himself in an effort to avoid pain. Torture is prima facie wrong because of the harm that it does, because it violates a person's autonomy, and because it deliberately injures a person who is defenseless and at our mercy (see Shue, 1978 and

Scarry, 1985). Since it is prima facie wrong, torture requires special justification.

Actions that might be called torture can be understood as having a family resemblance: there is a plurality of actions that might be called torture. This plurality includes actions that are more or less harmful, more or less deliberate, more or less in violation of the victim's autonomy, and more or less intended to distort, contort, and twist its victim. The more certain we are that an activity is torture, the stronger the normative content involved in calling it such. Obviously harmful, deliberate, and distorting treatment is prima facie wrong. The burden of proof rests upon the proponent of such an act, who has to show that such a presumptively wrong act can be morally justified by applying some sort of utilitarian calculus.

The concept of violence is closely related to torture. Indeed, some might say that the essence of torture is found in its violence. But violence is as fuzzy a concept as torture. Storms can be said to be violent; but so are criminals, institutions, and sneezes. These various things are related by family resemblance. Actions are violent (and harder to justify) to the degree that they are forceful, destructive, and occur in violation of autonomy. Thus, violence has been related etymologically both to *violentia* (a Latin word which can be translated as "vehemence") and to *violare* (a Latin word meaning violation or infringement). Regardless of which sense of violence we want to emphasize, it is clear that acts identified as violence are presumed to be wrong: and the more clearly they are violent, the more difficult it is to justify them.

Perhaps the biggest difference between violence and torture is the intended aim of distortion or twisting of the victim. A punch, slap, or knife thrust is violent; but these do not intend to distort the victim. But waterboarding does use the victim's reaction to panic, pain, and fear with the intention of turning the victim against himself—by asking him to betray himself, his associates, and his cause. Some of the most well-known examples of torture are found in the Inquisition, where the goal of torture was to twist the victim free of corruption and turn him back toward true faith. In this sense, torture was used to correct or rectify: it was a process by which a twisted soul was made straight. The current debate is not grounded in spiritualized interpretations of this sort. Indeed, in our secular society, spiritual uses of force are prohibited. And this is why the current debate is articulated primarily in utilitarian language that makes no claims about correcting the terrorist.

THE BURDEN OF PROOF AND VALUE CONFLICT

It is impossible to complete an ostensive list of acts of torture, since the human imagination is quite adept at creating ways of twisting human beings. At best, a list of tortures will be related by family resemblance. The next question, however, is about the logic and morality of such fuzzy terms. What sorts of principles should we employ when using such vague terms? There is no good answer to this question. Indeed, value conflict is reiterated at the level of definitional inquiry.

I generally argue that for a concept such as torture that has negative normative connotations, the burden of proof should rest on arguments for exclusion. In other words, since the concept identifies things that are presumed to be wrong, the burden rests on those who argue that a putative instance of torture is not really torture. Thus, those who argue that waterboarding is not torture should have to prove that it is not; the burden should not go the other way around. But my preference here reflects my preference for deontological prohibitions on violence and my sympathy for pacifism. Utilitarians and realists will not share my presumptions and preferences. The deontological and pacifist view takes seriously an expansive idea of torture: the family resemblance includes many activities grouped together because these activities are presumed to be harmful and to require special moral justification (if they can be justified at all). My approach is thus in line with what Vittorio Bufacchi calls in his discussion of violence, a "comprehensive conception" (Bufacchi, 2005). A comprehensive conception of violence includes of a wide range of phenomena such as institutional or structural violence. For deontologists who want to protect human beings from abuse and disrespect, a comprehensive conception is to be preferred. An action that is suspected of being torture or violence should be regarded as such until it can be shown not to be. If we are going to err in describing actions, the deontological standpoint wants to err on the side of protecting individuals from abuse.

History gives us good reason to take up a comprehensive and critical view of torture. The historical argument is grounded in the fact that human culture has generally been quite permissive regarding torture. We have allowed all sorts of horrible things to be done to human beings: from burning at the stake to genital mutilation. Often these activities were justified in the name of the common good. For much of human history the burden of proof rested upon the one who argued that these activities were negative, harmful, and unjust. For the Romans, while crucifixion was a horrible punishment, it was also not exorbitant, since the state could do whatever it thought was needed to defend the common good. We've made great progress since then. But we still accept violence as normal. For example, genital mutilation practiced on males in Western cultures (and on females in other cultures) is often viewed as a normal procedure and not viewed as a violent act in need of special justification. History reminds us that judicial (and religious and other cultural) activities that twist, distort, and manipulate human bodies are easily justified by defenders of the common good. There has been and will always be a risk that interrogations will employ torture. We know that religious authorities have used all sorts of means to keep sexuality in check, especially female sexuality. And we know that zealots will always feel the urge to correct the souls of those whom they believe to be spiritually distorted.

This historical context is important for determining the burden of proof. A more progressive moral sensibility should lead us to be more inclusive in identifying violent acts and acts of torture. Progress toward a more humane world will occur as we continue to expand the application of these negative normative concepts as far as they will comfortably stretch. Activities like waterboarding must be called torture so that we might be as careful as possible in thinking about their justification.

The problem is, however, that not everyone shares my deontological presupposition. Indeed, the debate about waterboarding and torture shows us that there is another side. Defenders of torture believe that if it works to defend the common good, it is obviously justifiable. And defenders of waterboarding believe that its harm is so minimal that it is not torture and it does not require special justification. Indeed, a defender of the common good might argue that it is up to the opponent of waterboarding to prove that it is torture and that it cannot be justified. The structural problem of definition and the burden of proof in justification thus reflects the conflict between deontological and utilitarian moral theories.

Political and rhetorical quibbling about the question of whether waterboarding is actually torture can distract us from the ethical question of whether coercive and violent techniques can ever be justified in defense of the common good. That may be the exact reason that this quibbling goes on: as a way of side-stepping the deeper issue. Those who advocate the use of waterboarding do not want to be seen as advocating torture or defending something that is immoral and so they try to claim that it is not torture. But let's note that on a strictly utilitarian point of view, torture is not wrong. It can easily be justified by utilitarian calculation in a ticking-bomb scenario—as described, for example, by Dershowitz (2002). Defenders of waterboarding who also want to claim that it is not torture are perhaps afraid to bite the utilitarian bullet and admit that in defense of the common good, individuals can be used and twisted.

DEONTOLOGICAL AND UTILITARIAN CONCERNS IN DEFINING VIOLENCE AND TORTURE

The *Encyclopedia of Ethics* defines torture as follows:

> The deliberate infliction of violence, and through violence, of severe mental and/or physical suffering upon individuals. It may be inflicted by individuals or groups and for diverse ends, ranging from extracting information, confession, admission of culpability or liability, and self-incrimination to general persuasion, intimidation, and amusement. (Becker and Becker, 2001, 1719)

The difficulty of this definition is that it relies upon the slippery concept of violence. The literature on violence shows us that the concept of violence is not exactly clear—especially at the margins. Is it violent to deprive you of water, or to keep you from sleeping, or to prevent you from using a toilet and so to cause you to defecate on yourself? Is it violent to play loud music or to subject you to isolation or to use stress positions or to waterboard you? There is a continuum here and violence remains a fuzzy family resemblance term. If we were clear about the concept of violence, then we might be clear about whether these sorts of activities were torture, according to this definition.

But before taking up a definition of violence, let me reiterate my own deontological presupposition. I argue that if we suspect that any of these activities are violent or are torture, then the burden of proof is on the one who denies this. There is a basic point here about nonmaleficence: we have a prima facie duty to do no harm.

There is nothing obviously wrong about providing water to someone who is thirsty—and so we would never suspect that giving water to the thirsty was torture or was violence. But depriving a person of water is different, as is dumping water over the face of someone who is strapped down on their back. We have good reasons to suspect that there is violence at work here. And so the burden appears to rest upon the one who denies this. Of course, simply identifying an act as violence or as torture tells us nothing about whether it is justified. Again, utilitarians will argue that some forms of violence and some uses of torture may be justifiable. Utilitarians can still hold that nonmaleficence is important even if harms can sometimes be justified in pursuit of the greater good, since minimizing harm is also part of the overall effort to maximize happiness. But deontologists give nonmaleficence a much deeper significance.

The difference between utilitarians and deontologists can be partially explained by the fact that the utilitarian is more willing to concede that manipulations of pleasure and pain will work to alter people's behavior and produce good outcomes. Thus, for utilitarians, nonmaleficence can give way to concern for the greater happiness, since small increments of harm can produce great benefits for the greater number. Deontologists are more suspicious of this sort of calculation. Not only do they hold that individuals should not be used in this way but they also tend to doubt that autonomous human beings can be so easily manipulated. This empirical and psychological difference is important. On the one hand, utilitarians tend to view human beings as animals that can be manipulated by strategic use of pain and pleasure. Bentham begins his *Principles of Moral and Legislation* as follows: "Nature has placed mankind under the governance of two sovereign masters, pain and pleasure." On the other hand, deontologists tend to view intention and will as primary. Kant begins his *Fundamental Principles of the Metaphysic of Morals* as follows: "It is impossible to conceive of anything anywhere in the world or even anywhere out of it that can be without qualification be called good, except a Good Will." Kantians tend to view human beings from the inside, as it were, as souls or persons with an inner life of autonomous intention, while utilitarians approach human beings from the outside as creatures to be manipulated by pleasure and pain. These two different approaches lead to divergent conclusions about who has to prove what in terms of the justification of torture.

Of course, we must be careful here in establishing this dichotomy. Kant and Bentham are not merely single-minded fanatics unaware of the complexity of human life. Deontologists and utilitarians recognize the subtlety of these sorts of discussions. Consider, for example, Mill's discussion of motive and intention in *Utilitarianism*. Mill explains that the "morality of the action" is based upon the consequences, while the "worth of the agent" is focused on the motive (Mill, 1998c, 150). Mill then considers, in a footnote, a case in which a tyrant rescues a man from drowning "in order that he might inflict upon him more exquisite tortures." This case begs to be compared with the case of waterboarding, since this is very similar to what happens in waterboarding: drowning is simulated and the victim is rescued in order to torture him again. Mill concludes that "he who saves another from drowning in order to kill him by torture afterwards, does not differ only in motive from him who does the same thing from duty or benevolence; the act itself is different." Mill concludes that "the morality of the action depends entirely upon the intention." This might seem to connect Mill to Kant. But what Mill seems to have in mind here is that the "intention" behind an action helps us to define the entirety of the action. If I save you in order to torture you, the act includes both the saving and the torturing (or at least that is how I intend the act). And this is how utilitarians understand the justification of torture. If the intention is not merely to inflict harm on the victim but also to save the innocent, then the act is benevolent and torture becomes justifiable.

At any rate, utilitarians remain more interested in consequences and the outcomes of actions, while deontologists are more interested in intentions and the inner aspect of actions. For the utilitarian, we would have to extend the scope of the action to include the goal for which we are using torture. Torture for amusement would be wrong, while interrogative torture appears to be justifiable. But for the deontologist, the scope of the action appears more narrow. The question for the deontologist is not whether good outcomes can be produced but whether the action expresses respect for human dignity. But the problem is that for a Kantian, torture does not respect human dignity since, by definition, its distorting and contorting manipulation is used in violation of human autonomy.

Before digging further into this difference, let's consider the larger concept, violence, since the term "violence" shows up in the definition of torture from the *Encyclopedia of Ethics*, quoted above. Like other contested terms in moral and political discourse, we think we know violence when we see it; but when pushed to give a precise analysis, we often end up in confusion. Violence can be used to describe institutional racism, domestic abuse, and murder. Violence is an important topic—perhaps one of the most important—for ethics and political philosophy. However, it is surprising how often the term is simply undefined. One recent example is Martha Nussbaum's excellent and provocative article, "Women's Bodies: Violence, Security, and Capabilities" (2005). Nussbaum provides gruesome details about violence against women and she shows how these acts threaten and undermine women's "capabilities" and flourishing. While this is compelling and important, one wonders exactly what it is that makes the list of crimes against women *violent*; or to return to OMCT, what makes them *torture*. To cite one borderline example, Nussbaum suggests that a woman who is infected with HIV by her husband, who lied to her about his infection, has suffered violence. This seems to be quite an extension of what we normally mean by violence. Rape is violence; but is it also violence to be secretly or even inadvertently infected by a sexually transmitted disease? The answer depends on how we define violence.

The seemingly obvious definitional matter of *what violence is* is closely related to the vexing normative question of *why violence is bad or wrong*. For the utilitarian, the presence of harm is enough to require justification. But deontologists will go further and claim that violence also violates autonomy and thus disrespects human dignity. The deontologist will also add that violence includes the intention to harm and to violate. Violence is thus a deliberate action of an agent that aims to harm another person in violation of their autonomy. This deontological language was seen in the definition of torture from the *Encyclopedia of Ethics* quoted above: torture is supposed to be "deliberate infliction of violence." But notice that this sort of definition is deontological in its emphasis on intention and autonomy.

With this sort of definition in mind, Nussbaum's case of the husband who infects his wife with HIV is on the borderline. Clearly, the husband has harmed his wife; and he may be condemned for that by a utilitarian. But the question of whether the husband was violent depends upon the question of whether the husband intended to harm the wife and deliberately set out to infect her. Such a case is quite different from forced prostitution or waterboarding—acts which can only be described with some mention of the intention of the pimp or the interrogator. The intentional aspect is important because violence is supposed to correlate to responsibility. Although we do talk about unwitting violence—this is an extension of our ordinary understanding of violence as a quality of the acts of agents who are responsible for their actions. The issue of responsibility is more important for the deontological perspective. Utilitarians are simply concerned with minimizing harm and maximizing happiness for the greater number. But deontologists are also concerned with assigning responsibility—and responsibility has to do with the intentions of the agent, not merely with the results of his actions.

SUBJECTIVITY AND HARM

A violent act is a deliberate action of an agent who aims to harm another person in violation of their autonomy. Torture, it would seem, could be defined in much the same way: as deliberate violence inflicted on a person with the intention of distortion. The main difference between violence in general and torture is the way that torture intends to twist and contort the human against himself. Torture's violence is specific: it is violence that intends to distort.

In stipulating this difference, we have to make use of the primarily deontological concept of intention and the deliberate effort to distort. By focusing on the intentional or deliberate character of the act, we bring in deontological concerns about human agency, autonomy, and responsibility. Torture does not happen by accident. It is done by responsible agents. And to be responsible in the sense I have in mind here, the agent must deliberately intend his act along with its consequences. If we try to avoid these deontological concerns, we end up with a definition, not of violence, but of "harm." If we ignore deliberate intention, the definition ends up as "violence is destructive force." This may suffice for a kind of basic utilitarianism, where the goal is simply to avoid harm and minimize destruction. But moral judgment also seems to require an inquiry into the agent's intentions and the victim's autonomy, as even Mill noted in his discussion of the "the worth of the agent."

We thus have to consider subjective aspects of the act if we are to be able to say with certainty when violence or torture has, in fact, been committed. Harms are easier to define objectively; but to say that violence or torture has occurred, we generally want to include some subjective element. However, if we allow violence to be defined in purely subjective terms, then all sorts of activities can appear to be violence or torture that we generally do not want to include here: from verbal abuse to divorce. Violence cannot simply be in the eye of the beholder. We do need objective criteria that can tell us when harms have occurred. And yet, violence also includes subjective elements such as the will of the "victim," the intentions of the perpetrator, etc. An objective fact of dentistry is that dentists sometimes harm teeth—say when they have to pull them or drill them; but we are also interested in whether the victim or patient wanted the teeth destroyed and whether the dentist intends to help or harm the patient. Actors and victims can be mistaken about harm: some actions that appear harmful may actually be beneficial and vice versa. An irrational fear of the dentist can lead one to think that the drill is harmful when it is really helping us. Thus, violence has an important subjective component because the perception of harm is also subjective, as is the intent of the perpetrator. Likewise, the perception of a violation of autonomy also contains a subjective element as well as an objective element. Some will claim, for example, that institutional racism violates their autonomy, others will not. While objective facts obviously matter here, there is an importantly subjective component in determining whether someone's dignity has been disrespected. Concern for these objective and subjective elements correlates to the concerns of deontological and utilitarian ethics. Deontologists are more concerned with subjectivity in the action—with the intention of the agent and the experienced violation of autonomy of the victim; and utilitarians are more concerned with objective harms.

And so to return to waterboarding. It is easy enough to see that it is violent because it uses force to harm its victim and it does so against his will. And it is an intentional act, deliberately aimed at producing panic and pain. It is torture insofar as it aims to distort its victim, coercing him into betraying himself or his cause. The subjective context matters here, since there are instances of waterboarding that are not violent or torture. Waterboarding has apparently been used in training soldiers as part of survival training. During the recent debate about waterboarding, some claimed that this proves that it is not torture, since it would be odd to claim that we would torture our own soldiers. But soldiers are also exposed to gas and explosions, etc. in order to train them to respond to attacks. When a soldier is waterboarded in training, the intention behind the act and the soldier's subjective response are quite different from when a defenseless detainee's head is forced under the water in a deliberate effort to turn him against himself.

CONCLUSION

This discussion of subjectivity and objectivity may help us interpret the Bybee memo of 2002. The Bybee memo focuses on the intensity of the pain and compares this to the objective occurrence of organ failure or death. This sort of analysis is focused on harm alone without concern for the intention of the interrogators, the perception of abuse on the part of the victim, the question of how the victim's autonomy is violated, or the issue of how the victim is distorted and turned against himself. In this sense, the Bybee memo indicates a purely utilitarian concern that is divorced from these sorts of deontological considerations. Further discussions of waterboarding and torture after the April 2009 release of the documentary evidence noted above indicate that the concern of the Bush Administration was purely utilitarian. In April 2009, former Vice-President Dick Cheney said quite simply that torture worked to prevent terrorist attacks. And he offered the very straightforward utilitarian justification of torture, quoted as the epilogue to this chapter.

If torture worked, then from the utilitarian perspective, it was a good thing. And Cheney maintains that no American President should foreswear the use of "enhanced interrogation" methods, since these have proved useful in preventing terrorism. This point of view is not concerned with cruelty or malicious intent. Nor is it concerned with the victim's suffering or with how the victim is distorted. In this sense, the utilitarian point of view is abstract and impersonal. It is concerned with the public good and not with these other more private moral concerns. And in fact, we do want our leaders to adopt this abstract utilitarian point of view: they should concern themselves with protecting the common good.

The importance of this abstract point of view helps to explain why Bentham imagined a whipping machine, as discussed in the last chapter. Torture need not be employed by sadistic psychopaths. Indeed, sadistic psychopaths will have a tendency to misuse torture. In his recent speech, Cheney condemned the sadistic torture at Abu Ghraib as an aberration that has no connection to the use of "enhanced interrogation" against KSM and other high-level terrorists. Critics will claim that this is a deliberate obfuscation, since the events at Abu Ghraib were at least facilitated by the permissive atmosphere in which "the gloves had come off," so to speak. But Cheney reminds us that the utilitarian justification of torture is not sadistic. Sadism is not as useful as carefully calibrated administration of pain, panic, and distorting manipulation. Cheney would seem to agree with Bentham that an abstract torture machine would be a useful improvement, especially if it could be used in such a way that the pain inflicted on the victim were measured and minimized, while also protecting the administrators of torture from adverse psychological reactions. For the utilitarian, what matters is the result. If pain that is administered by an impersonal machine produces good results, then this is progress. This reminds us that from the utilitarian point of view, the torturer himself is not considered as a person. Rather, he is a functionary of the state administering pain in defense of the common good. This way of thinking disturbs critics such as Derrick Jeffreys (and myself), as discussed in the previous chapter, since it is inherently dehumanizing. But for the utilitarian, the conclusion is obvious: if torture makes us safer, whether administered by functionaries, by sadists, or by machines, then it should be used.

Deontologists view things otherwise. They are concerned with the psyche of the torturer and the victim. Recall that Kant held that although murderers could be executed, they could not be abused. The point is that we must respect the dignity of persons, even terrorists—even as we fight them. Of course, deontological ethics suffers from difficulties as well. One difficulty here is that our intentions are not always clear, even to ourselves. It is possible to convince oneself that a violent act was not intentional: as when American interrogators "accidentally" killed detainees in Afghanistan by beating them to death.[3] Self-deception and false-consciousness are always possible. At least the utilitarian approach is willing to recognize harms in an objective sense and connect them with objective benefits in the utilitarian calculus. Unfortunately, this coldly objective approach overlooks the human interior of action. These two approaches cannot be reconciled.

NOTES

1. From the OMCT website: www.omct.org/index.php?id=EQL&lang=eng
2. Available at Human Rights First: www.humanrightsfirst.org/us_law/ etn/gonzales/memos_dir/memo_20020801_JD_%20Gonz_.pdf
3. See the summary report by the ACLU: www.aclu.org/intlhumanrights/ gen/21236prs20051024.html

CHAPTER ELEVEN

CONSCIENTIOUS REFUSAL AND THE LIBERAL TRADITION

No person religiously scrupulous of bearing arms shall be compelled to bear arms in person.
            James Madison, Proposed Addendum to the Second Amendment to the U.S. Constitution

After the Second World War and the trials at Nuremburg, it has become commonplace to maintain that soldiers can and should disobey immoral orders. Unfortunately, soldiers are still prosecuted for disobedience—even disobedience that is grounded in moral claims about the justice of a war. Such was the case of soldiers, like Pablo Paredes and Ehren Watada—who refused to deploy to the war in Iraq. These cases remind us of the tension between obedience and conscientious refusal.

The ideal of obedience does not fit well within the modern liberal tradition that begins with John Locke. Prior to Locke, obedience was presumed under something like the divine right of kings: if sovereign power comes from God, then obedience to the state is a religious requirement. Even Socrates imbued the Laws of the city with a kind of majesty that demanded obedience. During the Reformation, these sorts of ideas became harder to support. But it was not until Locke in the late-seventeenth century that we get a liberal theory of the state that includes the right to revolution and broad exceptions for religious toleration. The idea of conscientious objection develops primarily among thinkers that follow Locke. This idea extends even to soldiers. As the English abolitionist and critic of British colonial power, Granville Sharp, put it in 1773, "Even in public military Service, or warlike Expeditions by National Authority, the Law manifestly requires the Soldier to think for himself; and to consider, before he acts in any war, whether the same be just" (Sharp, 1773, 66).

Sharp defended liberty against slavery; and he was a British conscientious objector against the war against the American colonies. Sharp had also argued against the impressment of sailors—the practice of capturing able-bodied men and pressing them into naval service. Sharp's ideas had some influence on the American revolutionaries—he is, for example, credited with turning Benjamin Franklin against slavery (see Fruchtman, 2005). And indeed, Franklin claimed that the impressment of seamen was akin to slavery: "there being no slavery worse than that sailors are subjected to" (Franklin, 1836, 334). The issue of impressment had sparked riots in New England throughout the eighteenth century; it was one of the causes that fueled the American Revolution; and it certainly contributed to the war of 1812.

Forced military service on a mass scale came into its own in the twentieth century, with the rise of the mass army. In the United States, conscription and the draft were instituted during the First World War with the Conscription Act of 1917. President Woodrow Wilson defended this law with sweeping claims about the common good in his speech of May 28, 1917. Wilson claimed that the people must join together against the common foe. And he went on:

> But this cannot be if each man pursues a private purpose. All must pursue one purpose. The nation needs all men; but it needs each man not in the field that will most pleasure him, but in the endeavour that will best serve the common good.

The idea that the common good required involuntary service was used repeatedly to support both wartime and peacetime drafts. Exemptions were carved out for conscientious objectors, who ended up in alternative service such as that provided by the Civilian Public Service camps during the Second World War (Flynn, 1989; and Zahn, 1989). But the idea that the common good required forced military service continued to be widely held until the draft was abolished in the 1970s under President Ford. Despite the fact that the United States has turned to an all-volunteer army, young men in the United States are still required to register with the Selective Service, in case a draft is again required in defense of the common good. And volunteer soldiers such as Paredes and Watada are expected to obey.

Conscientious objectors and draft resisters will argue that no one should be forced to subvert their consciences, even in defense of the common good. Moreover, critics will argue that the idea of the "common good" is not clearly defined. And when it appears that the state is acting unjustly, conscientious objectors will argue that disobedience is morally required. In the twentieth century, the best-known defender of the idea of conscientious refusal is Martin Luther King Jr. King argued for this idea in his "Letter from Birmingham Jail," where he concluded that "one has a moral responsibility to disobey unjust laws" (King, 1963, 3). King connects his idea to Socrates and to Jesus. And he claimed that this idea has roots in ideas of Augustine, Aquinas, and others in the natural law tradition. According to King, this tradition holds that "An unjust law is no law at all." But King overestimates this tradition. Socrates and Jesus both eventually submitted to state power, while the medieval natural law tradition tends to hold that obedience to higher power is required. It is the liberal theory of human rights that establishes human autonomy and private conscience as a bastion of liberty in opposition to the state.

On the liberal view, there is no legal duty to fight in an illegal war and no moral duty to fight in an immoral war. Indeed, a state that requires immoral service or demands that individuals act in violation of their private consciences is unjust. The liberal tradition holds that unjust states can (and perhaps *should*) be disobeyed, even to the point of revolution.

THE ENLIGHTENMENT

Modern liberalism takes hold during the Enlightenment, which gave rise to the American and French Revolutions. The most influential philosopher of the Enlightenment is Kant. But in some respects, Kant's views do not go far enough. This is especially true with regard to the question of obedience and conscientious objection. Kant maintains that public officials may argue against state policies in "public"—that is, in the press or some other public venue. But at the end of the day, public officials must obey. This idea was formulated in Kant's essay, "What is Enlightenment?" from 1784. Kant thought that the Prussian state in the 1780s was an "enlightened"

one under Frederick the Great. Obedience was owed to the enlightened state, since it guaranteed freedom of expression in the public
sphere. Indeed, Kant affirmed a categorical imperative of obedience: "Obey the suzerain (in everything that does not conflict with
internal morality) who has authority over you!" (Kant, 1965b, 139).
This passage has troubled many interpreters. But the consensus is
that Kant maintains, as Dostal puts it, "the individual citizen does
not have the right to decide that a certain war is immoral and thus
cannot justifiably refuse to be conscripted" (Dostal, 2001, 144).

Kant's ideas can be connected to our previous discussion of
professional ethics. Even though political professionals and public
servants—soldiers, diplomats, and even public school teachers—
might disagree with a policy, Kant maintains that their professional duty is to remain obedient. The remedy for bad policy is
found in the political right to question and criticize, which is the
hallmark of the "enlightened" state. Kant's conclusion in "What is
Enlightenment?" is: *argue as much as you like about whatever you
like, but obey* (Kant, 1991e, 59). The important caveat is that this
holds only as long as the state is enlightened, that is, so long as it
actually allows the free exercise of public reason as the remedy for
bad policy. This idea has much in common with an argument made
recently by David Estlund, who holds that soldiers should obey so
long as they are sure the state and the war are just (Estlund, 2007).
One sign of an enlightened state would be its democratic approach
to the question of war: an enlightened state should ask its citizens—
and thus its citizen-soldiers—to consent to war.

Frederick the Great died in 1786 and was replaced by the less
enlightened monarch, Frederick Wilhelm II. Frederick Wilhelm
was a reactionary who cracked down upon dissent as part of a
general European conservative backlash against the revolutionary
fervor that came to a climax with the French Revolution. In 1794,
Kant ran into trouble with Frederick Wilhelm's censors. When the
censors condemned Kant's humanistic religious writings, Kant
promised not to publish anything further on religion. But when
Frederick Wilhelm II died in 1797, Kant viewed himself as free
of that promise and proceeded to publish his final reflections on
religion.

This episode reminds us that context and circumstance matter when thinking about obedience and conscientious objection.
Kant appeared not to have any desire for revolution or political

confrontation, perhaps because this episode unfolded toward the end of his life. After working at the University of Königsberg throughout his life, Kant was in his 70s when he ran afoul of the censors. At that point in life, the option of going elsewhere or staging a revolution was unappealing to Kant, as it was to Socrates, Galileo, and other wise old men whose ideas lead them into conflict with authority. This kind of passivity can appear to be odd to us today—especially to those of us committed to the basic ideas of the liberal tradition. But in a certain context, at a certain point in life, obedience may appear more prudent than disobedience or revolution. Moreover, Kant's basic ethical framework focused on duty, obedience, and promise keeping. Indeed, the same can be said of Galileo and Socrates. These were morally upright men, whose moral compunction prevented them from running away or from taking more radical action. This sort of obedience is admirable in its own way. But, as critics will note, there is little inspiration here for those who aspire to more radical political action.

Perhaps it is true that revolutionary activity, civil disobedience, and conscientious objection are really the province of the youth. But more likely, those who are driven to conscientious objection and civil disobedience are so moved by outrage over injustice that they can no longer passively and obediently accept the status quo. Consider Kant's contemporary, Granville Sharp, whom we discussed above. In 1776, Sharp resigned his position in the British Ordinance department in protest against the war against the colonists—Sharp was in his 40s at the time. Sharp used his newfound freedom from government service to continue his efforts against slavery, an effort that culminated in the abolition of slavery in England in 1807.

The idea of conscientious objection and civil disobedience is more easily grounded in the Anglo-American tradition than in the Kantian or Germanic tradition. The liberal view of the state found in the Anglo-American tradition holds that individuals have basic rights over against the state and even that the people retain a right to revolution when the state infringes upon these rights. The basic idea is that human beings are endowed with inalienable rights including: the right to life, liberty, property, and happiness. When this view is taken seriously, it becomes difficult to see how compulsory military service is possible, since compulsory military service transfers the right to life and liberty over to the state.

It also becomes difficult on this view to defend the doctrine of slavery, since slavery is another obvious violation of liberty. Indeed, conscription and slavery have much in common, as Franklin noted. This same conjunction of antiwar and antislavery ideals is found in the ideas of other Americans such as Emerson and especially Thoreau. As we shall see, a similar conjunction of ideas worked in tandem in the civil rights and antiwar movements of the 1960s.

It is not surprising that ideas about conscientious refusal developed in the United States. Many of the American colonists had migrated to the New World in pursuit of religious liberty. And some of the Americans held religious views that were opposed to war. Pennsylvania, for example, was founded by the Quaker pacifist, William Penn. Like Locke, Penn and others, such as Roger Williams, the founder of Rhode Island, also argued in favor of religious toleration (see Nussbaum, 2008). For Williams and Penn, Christianity was a religion of peace and Christians should be opposed to war and to the use of force in religious matters. Even during the Revolution, Americans had to find a way to accommodate Quakers, Mennonites, and others who were prohibited by religion from bearing arms. On July 18, 1775, the Continental Congress included the possibility of conscientious objection in its call for the formation of militias of "minute men." James Madison, George Washington, and others of the Founders agreed with the basic idea and tried to find ways to accommodate conscientious objectors. At the constitutional convention for the state of Virginia, Madison lobbied to provide for extensive rights of conscientious refusal, "unless the preservation of equal liberty and the existence of the State are manifestly endangered" (Ketcham, 1990, 73; cf. Nussbaum, 2008, 122). And Madison campaigned to have a similar exemption included in the Second Amendment: "no person religiously scrupulous of bearing arms shall be compelled to bear arms in person" (quoted in Noone, 1989, 2).

These sorts of ideas were brought together with polemical force by Thoreau in his essay on disobedience—an essay that influenced thinkers and political activists from Tolstoy and Gandhi to King. Thoreau's defense of private conscience leads to a radical critique of state power and the claim that unjust laws should be transgressed at once. Thoreau maintains that his doctrine of civil disobedience is grounded on the right to revolution. "All men recognize the right of revolution; that is, the right to refuse allegiance to, and to resist, the government, when its tyranny or its inefficiency are great and unendurable" (Thoreau, 2000b, 670–671). This passage echoes themes found in the Declaration of Independence and prior to that in Locke. Thoreau's basic view is that "That government is best which governs not at all." He sees the state as a necessary evil that should whither away and die. He also claims that standing armies are evil because they can be perverted and used for evil purposes by the standing government.

Thoreau offered these reflections in the 1840s during the Mexican-American war and was willing to go to jail as a result of his refusal to pay war taxes. Although Thoreau would seem to agree with Kant's ideas about autonomy and his critique of standing armies, Thoreau takes these ideas to another level of practical and radical application. Thoreau is not afraid of the revolutionary energy implicit in his approach. He recalled that the American system begins in revolution. And Thoreau believed that a revolution would be needed to eradicate the evil of slavery. Unlike Kant, Thoreau's advocacy of autonomy and private conscience was not limited by concern for public order. Indeed, Thoreau and those who follow him, such as King, hold that when the public order is grounded on injustice, it is in fact time for revolution.

Thoreau famously criticized military service for producing wooden men who serve the state, "not as men mainly, but as machines, with their bodies" because they are not permitted "free exercise of the judgment of the moral sense" (Thoreau, 2000b, 669–670). Kant also wanted soldiers to remain men. He maintained that soldiers should argue but obey. Thoreau goes further. He implies that soldiers should question and resist. There are good reasons to take Kant's view seriously—indeed it appears to be the mainstream view in contemporary democratic societies. But Thoreau's view is better. Soldiers should be encouraged to make judgments about the justice of war. And when they believe that a war is unjust, they should be encouraged to act upon that judgment by refusing to serve.

VIETNAM, RAWLS, AND KING

In the 1960s, in protests against the Vietnam War, young Americans burned draft cards or fled the country. In protests against this unjust war, conscientious objection became an important tool. And conscientious objection and civil disobedience became hallmarks of both the peace movement and the civil rights movement.

The hope of pacifists is that someday there would be a world in which people will simply choose not to fight wars. Carl Sandburg coined the phrase: "Sometime they'll give a war and nobody will come" in his poem, "Little Girl Saw Her First Troop Parade." We do not yet live in a world where this is possible. But we are making progress. And one way to make further progress would be to take seriously a slight alteration to the pacifist slogan: "Someday they'll give an *unjust* war and nobody will come." If we could empower soldiers not to fight in wars that are unjust, we would be making a giant step in the right direction. If soldiers were given this power, there would be far fewer wars and the wars that were fought would tend to be more just.

During the 1960s there was a substantial discourse about this question. Some important legal cases helped to clarify the idea of conscientious objection. Perhaps the most famous case of conscientious objection was that of the boxer, Mohammad Ali. Ali's application for conscientious objector status was refused and after Ali appealed, it made its way to the Supreme Court. At issue here was the question of whether Ali's refusal was merely political or sincerely religious. Ali's conversion to the Nation of Islam movement under Elijah Mohammad—including his name change from Cassius Clay to Mohammad Ali—was seen as a political move prompted by the radical black politics of the 1960s. The Department of Justice viewed Ali's refusal as "political and racial" and thus not as sincerely religious. The Court sided with Ali against the Justice Department and held that his objection to service was broad and sincere enough to qualify for conscientious objector status. "For the record shows that the petitioner's beliefs are founded on tenets of the Muslim religion as he understands them" (*Clay v. U.S.*, 1971). The Court recognized that one is entitled to interpret religious tradition according to one's own understanding and refuse military service based on this private interpretation.

This summarized the developed view of conscientious objection after the cases of Daniel Seeger in 1965 and Elliott Welsh in 1970—both of which were cited as precedents in the Clay (Ali) case. These cases broadened the conception of conscientious refusal—from an explicitly religious exception grounded in the theology of traditional Christian peace churches to a more broadly construed moral objection to war. Instead of appealing to the official dogmas of an organized religion as the basis for conscientious objection, these individuals argued that conscientious refusal can also be grounded in basic ethical beliefs. Seeger had explained his own views as follows: "I have concluded that war, from the practical standpoint, is futile and self-defeating, and that, from the more important moral standpoint, it is unethical" (quoted in *Welsh v. U.S.*, 1970). The Court held in the Welsh case that conscientious objector status could be granted to people whose "consciences, spurred by deeply held moral, ethical or religious beliefs would give them no rest or peace if they allowed themselves to become a part of an instrument of war" (*Welsh v. U.S.*, 1970). Thus, during the Vietnam era, conscientious refusal was expanded from a purely religious exemption of the sort envisioned by the Founders toward a moral refusal that could be grounded in just war ideas. And this extended far enough to include conscientious objection for a black Muslim like Muhammad Ali.

With this sort of moral exemption in place it becomes possible to defend "selective conscientious objection." Selective refusal is different from outright pacifism. Absolute pacifists will argue that war in general is wrong. But selective conscientious objection holds only that a particular war is wrong. This idea has been discussed and defended by a variety of authors including, most significantly, John Rawls, who links it to a form of "contingent pacifism." According to Rawls, not only may a soldier refuse to fight in a war that he judges to be unjust, but also: "If the aims of the conflict are sufficiently dubious and the likelihood of receiving flagrantly unjust commands is sufficiently great, one may have a *duty* and not only a right to refuse" (Rawls, 1971, 38; emphasis added). Rawls continues to say that in this day and age (he is writing in the midst of the Vietnam War), large and powerful states are "so likely to be unjust that one is forced to conclude that in the foreseeable future one must abjure military service altogether." Rawls concludes that systematic conscientious refusal would be useful since it would make the continuation of an unjust war "impossible."

This theory was put into practice by antiwar protesters, who shared strategies and goals with civil rights protesters. Martin Luther King, for example, encouraged conscientious objection to the draft and expressed his admiration for those, like Muhammad

Ali, who were willing to risk prison in objection to the war (see Jackson, 2007, 324). King directly linked the civil rights movement to the antiwar movement in his sermon "Beyond Vietnam," where he argued that at some point it became necessary to say no to war. According to King, silence is betrayal. While it is easy to acquiesce and comply with the status quo, King appears to agree with Rawls that we have a duty to oppose an unjust war. King took up Thoreau's idea that one should be a "counter-friction to the machine." When the war machine leads to gross injustice, it is wrong to remain silent. King calls for a complete reordering of our priorities so that the pursuit of peace takes precedence over pursuit of war and power. But King notes that we fail to react because of comfort and complacency. We adjust to injustice and try to avoid actions that could lead to revolution. But for King, civil rights violations and war are both such systematic problems, that some kind of revolution is required. As King famously put it in his sermon on Vietnam, it is not enough simply to be a Good Samaritan; you also have to transform the whole Jericho Road so that the system is revolutionized. One way to create this sort of transformation is via conscientious refusal.

THE VOLUNTEER ARMY AND CIVILIAN CONTROL

The idea of asking soldiers whether they want to fight sounds absurd to those who believe either that the military requires blind obedience or that military personnel are belligerent conformists. But the modern professional military is made up of principled volunteers. After Vietnam, in reaction to the draft resistance and conscientious objection movements of the 1960s, conscripted military service was eliminated in the United States. And the volunteer, professional army has proved to be strong and powerful. It is odd, however, that in a volunteer army, selective refusal is not permitted. One would think that a volunteer would be permitted to quit or to refuse to serve.

Since Nuremburg, the military allows for selective disobedience to immoral commands. The American officer corps in the post-Vietnam era is both sensitive to and knowledgeable about military ethics and the requirements of just war theory. The Mai Lai massacre is often studied and Hugh Thompson—the American helicopter pilot who stopped the massacre—was awarded the Soldier's Medal in 1998, along with his comrades, Glenn Andreotta and Lawrence Colburn. There is some resonance between Vietnam, the Mai Lai massacre, and the war in Iraq. Indeed, at least one key player was involved in both—early in his career Secretary of State Colin Powell was the officer in charge of investigating the Mai Lai massacre. At any rate, before and during the Iraq war, many officers were deeply disturbed by the moral problem presented by the war. Eventually this culminated in the so-called revolt of the generals—the group of senior officers who denounced Donald Rumsfeld in 2006 (see Cook, 2008). This "revolt" had both moral and practical components. It was partly about the justification of the war and partly about how the war was conducted. But this nature of this "revolt" shows us the problem: active duty generals could not refuse to obey the civilian leadership; so it was retired generals who spoke out.

The American military does not currently have a mechanism for selective refusal. But selective conscientious objection could easily be institutionalized. Indeed, some nations—such as the Netherlands—do allow for selective conscientious objection.[1] Professional soldiers volunteer to fight just wars in defense of principles of justice and human rights. There is no good reason to force them to fight in wars that they do not believe meet this standard. To do so would violate their autonomy and would treat them as mere means in the way that Kant criticized. And on a more mundane and prudent level, it is likely that an army will fight better without conscientious objectors in service: morale and unit cohesion suffer when disgruntled objectors are forced to serve.

We should encourage soldiers to make moral judgments about the justness of particular wars. Principled moral disagreement should not require them to break the law or their professional code. Rather, judicious moral judgment about *jus ad bellum* should be one of the obligations of the military profession. Senior officers, especially, would presumably be in a very good position to make such judgments, since they have the education, the experience, and the expertise to judge well about such things. Furthermore, it would be difficult to accuse a senior officer of merely being a coward or a malingerer. Selective conscientious objection is not a way for an officer to shirk his duty; rather it is a way to express a principled disagreement with the morality of a particular war. And pragmatically speaking, senior officers should wholeheartedly agree with the war they are asked to fight, so that they might motivate their men to take up the cause and fight well.

The American military only provides for conscientious objection based upon a total commitment to pacifism that is linked to religious belief. So, if a soldier has a religious conversion during the course of his enlistment, he could opt out. But a soldier may not refuse to fight in a given war on principled nonpacifist grounds. In reality most people are not absolute pacifists (and the number of sincere absolute pacifists in the volunteer army must be miniscule). So there should be a mechanism that allows for principled conscientious refusal short of complete pacifism.

One objection to this idea is that conscientious refusal will run counter to the democratic ideal of civilian control of the military. Related to this is the claim that consensus or unanimity of opinion is too much to ask for complex political decisions such as the decision to go to war. We elect our officials to make difficult decisions. Soldiers sign on to obey those decisions and the Constitutional system that legitimates these decisions. Once the decision has been made to go to war, it seems that we need the unanimous support of the military and obedience to the principle of democratic/civilian control. Insubordination may seem to be a sort of mutiny that undermines the important democratic principle of civilian control. Indeed, there are revolutionary implications here—as noted in our discussion of Thoreau and King.

Of course, it is not revolution that we want—but justice. Short of revolution, there should be a moral feedback loop based on just war principles between the military and the government. One reason for this is that military personnel still remain citizens and, as Kant says, they are "co-legislators." But unlike the rest of the citizenry, soldiers bear the moral, physical, and psychological burden of fighting. Certainly military personnel should not be allowed to refuse whenever they want for reasons that are arbitrary or morally insignificant. But they should be allowed to choose not to fight when their decision can be shown to be adequately grounded in just war principles.

Please note that this would only be a right to refuse. It would be too dangerous to allow military personnel to decide for themselves when to go to war. We could end up with a "Dr. Strangelove" situation in which the military launches a war on its own authority.

The point here is to limit war and to make it harder to fight unjust wars. So the selective disobedience I'm arguing for should only be about disobeying an order to go to war (and not about disobeying an order to abstain from war).

The option of selective conscientious objection would most likely not be widely employed. Volunteer soldiers want to fight in wars and refusal would get in the way of career advancement. Since Tocqueville, it has been widely recognized that the way to advance in a democratic army is through battle. Soldiers prepare for war, their careers are advanced by going to war, and they are willing to fight when the cause is just. So, if a war is obviously just, there will be very few objectors and the war will proceed. But if a war is questionable, then the numbers of refusals will increase. The more the war is suspected of injustice, the larger the number of refusals. This is, I argue, a useful feedback mechanism, as it will give all of us a sign as to the justice of the war. Civilian authorities would be wise to take the feedback of conscientious objectors about the morality of a war quite seriously. Indeed, democratic militaries should tolerate a more vigorous moral feedback loop in which soldiers—especially senior officers—are empowered to express their judgments about the morality of wars they are asked to fight.

After Nuremburg and more contemporary atrocities such as occurred at Mai Lai, it is a well established principle of modern armies that soldiers have the right to refuse immoral orders within war. It is fairly obvious that a soldier should disobey an order to shoot infants, poison a water supply, or engage in rape. But it is not so obvious what a soldier should do when he disagrees with the *ad bellum* judgment about the overall justness of the war. The difficulty of this question has to do with the general difficulty of making judgments about *jus ad bellum*. Larry May put it this way recently: "If it is difficult for theorists, many years after the fact, to determine whether a State had just cause to wage war, we cannot reasonably expect soldiers during wartime to make such a determination" (May, 2007, 30). Judgments about *jus ad bellum* are very difficult to make: they are based upon imperfect information and they are fraught with political complication, historical complexity, and uncertainty. Thus the burden of proof should be high here. Obedience to legitimate authority is an important value of the military and disobedience has a revolutionary trajectory. Thus the requirement of obedience should only be overridden when it is obvious that there is a serious breach of the principles of *jus ad bellum*. And even then, it is up to the soldier to prove his case against the government's *ad bellum* decision.

The ordinary soldier is not himself responsible for the *ad bellum* decision. Rather, the state or society as a whole is responsible for the *ad bellum* judgment. In a democracy, all citizens bear the burden of responsibility for *ad bellum* decisions *equally*: soldiers bear no more responsibility for going to war than the rest of the society, which sends them to war. Soldiers do bear more responsibility for making good judgment about *in bello* actions. But they are no more responsible for *ad bellum* decisions than any other voter. At the same time, however, soldiers bear the burden of service in a way that other voters do not. This unequal burden should make us more sensitive to the claims of soldiers who want to opt out of a putatively unjust war. Those who bear the burdens are entitled to decide if they think the burden is morally appropriate. If we fail to recognize this, we end up treating the soldier as a means and disrespecting his autonomy.

CONCLUSION

Hope that an enlightened state will respond to critique is one of the reasons that Kant thinks it is reasonable to "argue but obey." The hopeful idealism of Kant's "argue but obey" approach gives us an incentive to make sure that our institutions are just. If obedience to the institutions of professional life—including the military—is morally required, then citizens should aim to ensure that these institutions are as just as possible. But the history of the twentieth century reminds us that our institutions often fail to live up to the Enlightenment ideal. Sometimes the state does wrong—and in those cases, obedience is a vice and disobedience is a virtue.

There are several virtues of selective conscientious objection. First, it expresses respect for autonomy and prevents us from treating unwilling soldiers as mere means. Second, it coheres with basic principles of liberal democracy. Third, it helps principled military personnel to prevent the state from fighting unjust wars. And fourth, it provides a way to ensure the cohesion of the fighting unit. For these reasons, conscientious objection remains an important component of liberal democratic state. The expansion of conscientious objection even to include selective conscientious objection within the all-volunteer army would be a further step in the right direction.

NOTE

1. For country-by-country details see the UN Commission on Human Rights report, "The question of conscientious objection to military service" (1997): (www.hri.ca/fortherecord1997/documentation/commission/e-cn4–1997-99.htm).

CHAPTER TWELVE

PUBLIC MYTHS AND PRIVATE PROTEST

Has a philosopher like you failed to discover that our country is more to be valued and higher and holier far than mother or father or any ancestor?

Plato, Crito

Our lives are oriented around powerful myths. These myths often create a *Weltanschauung* that prevents critical thought. The most poignant example of this problem is found in Socrates' dialogue with Crito. Socrates imagines the Laws of Athens appearing to him and interrogating him, as he considers whether to run away from Athens in order to avoid execution. The Laws assert themselves as quoted in the epilogue to this chapter, claiming that they are more worthy of honor and obedience than any mortal mother or father. They continue to claim that obedience is required in military service and in other aspects of political life. They conclude by saying that if an individual should "do no violence to his father or mother, much less may he do violence to his country" (Plato, 1989, 51).

This mythic construction of the majesty of the law apparently leads Socrates to obey the law. And so he goes on to drink the hemlock and die. The layers of mythological illusion are striking in this passage. For one, the Laws appear as personified. And then the Laws themselves use an analogy with parenting and begetting that further undermines clear thinking. The Laws claim they deserve more honor than one's own parents, since the Laws themselves provided for and supported the human parents who give birth to the individual. But the problem is that it is not clear that evil parents deserve obedience; nor is it clear that a corrupt set of Laws can require our allegiance. Eloquent mythmaking can obscure this critical point—something that Plato indicates indirectly by show-ing us how even Socrates succumbed to an idealistic vision of the state.

Similar myths and analogies are used by Augustine to defend the use of violence. Augustine's reflections on violence and war are built upon a sustained interpretation of Scripture. He also uses common sense analogies to ground his reasoning. In the *City of God*, Augustine claims that the sovereign's duty to defend his peo-ple is similar to a father's duty to defend his children. And in his "Letter to Vincentius" he claims that a mother is entitled to use force to rebuke and discipline her children in order to keep them in line. Augustine maintains that violent force against heretics could be justified in this way, as well as by analogy with the way that the "good shepherd" uses his rod to keep the flock together. He then justifies discipline and violence with a maternal analogy.

> Whatever therefore the true and rightful Mother does, even when something severe and bitter is felt by her children at her hands, she is not rendering evil for evil, but is applying the benefit of discipline to counteract the evil of sin, not with the hatred which seeks to harm, but with the love which seeks to heal. (Augustine, 408)

This sort of account is central to any Christian justification of viol-ence. Violence is to be employed in a motherly fashion, as a love which seeks to heal. And thus the Church continued to exercise its motherly love against heretics and nonbelievers through the Crusades, the Inquisition, and the conquest of the Americas.

What is interesting in these passages from Plato and Augustine is the use of the parental analogy. It is easy to think that the state is like a parent. And if this analogy is accepted, along with other basic ethical ideas about revering one's parents, then obedience and loyalty are easily defended. But further reflection shows us that the analogy is so weak as to be absurd. The state is simply not another sort of parent; and the church is not simply another sort of mother. Our actual fathers and mothers know us as individuals. But large public institutions—such as churches and states—cannot deal with us as individuals. Rather, from the public standpoint, individuals are merely members of the whole. It is true that the public good can be grounded indirectly in the good of the individuals who make up the collective. But this grounding also grinds down upon individuals. Mythic analogies appear to ignore this problem.

THE JUST WAR MYTH

Similar myths continue to cloud clear thinking today. One of the most powerful contemporary myths is the idea that democracy is unequivocally good. When tied to faith in the idea that just wars are easy to fight, we end up with a powerful mythic ideal that has led to a variety of wars. Mythological idealism can be found in Enlightenment ideas about "civilization": the myth holds that modern Western civilization has such an unquestionable and universal value that it should be spread—by force if necessary—across the globe. Crusading idealists tend to think that the rest of the unenlightened world needs to be brought forcefully into the light provided by democracy and civilization. Idealism becomes dangerous when wars are fought in pursuit of the mythic ideal.

War is rarely just. The problem of what I call "the myth of the just war" is that if we believe that war is easily justified, we will tend to fight more wars. The just war myth is a socially constructed ideal that is supported by social institutions and that in turn helps to prop up those same social institutions. This is especially true in countries that have standing armies and long traditions of military intervention. Kant noted in *Perpetual Peace* that just war theories—such as those developed by Grotius and other "notable men"—are misused by politicians who pay lip service to the ideal of justice, while pursuing power at the expense of morality (Kant, 1991d, 103). I fear that this remains true today.

The danger of the just war ideal is that it often functions to insulate war from criticism. One need only recall the paradigm that developed in thinking about the Second World War as the "good war." But this war was not obviously just: the United States violated principles of *jus in bello* in the bombing campaigns against Japan, which culminated in the atomic bombing of Hiroshima and Nagasaki. Similar atrocities occurred in Europe: American and British bombers were indiscriminate killers; and Russian troops raped and pillaged in retaliation against the Nazis. The myth of the just war either makes it easy to overlook the incineration of Japanese and German children, or it allows us to justify these deaths by using a gross utilitarian calculation. A similar sort of idealism has been at the heart of the war on terrorism, which many initially supported as a just war in response to a belligerent enemy that would also help to spread democracy and civilization.

The democratizing myth has been used to support a variety of wars. American soldiers settled the West, destroying native cultures along the way—under the banner of civilization. The United States carried its "white man's burden" forward in wars that culminated in the annexation of Hawaii and far flung territories from Cuba and Puerto Rico to the Philippines. American forces entered the First World War in order to make the world safe for democracy. Allied forces fought against fascism in an effort to defend liberty and democracy. Then the Free World engaged in a nuclear arms race and fought several hot wars during the Cold War period in an effort to prevent the dominoes of Communism from falling. More recently, the United States invaded Iraq in an effort to eliminate a tyrant and establish democracy by force.

In each case, there were moral problems in the way that the democratizing ideal was carried out. Through the twentieth century, forces of democracy used poison gas, carpet bombing, atomic bombing, and the strategy of mutually assured destruction. And in the war on terrorism, democratizing forces have mounted aggressive wars aimed at regime change; they have used cluster bombs and high-altitude bombing, and they have employed torture. In each of these cases, democratizing forces have failed to live up to the standards of the just war theory.

What is more significant and more troubling is that despite these moral failings, these democratic wars have had broad public support. The public happily supports wars that fail to live up to the standard. Mythic idealism prevents us from seeing the immorality of the means we employ. We celebrate Allied victory in the Second World War, while failing to see the atrocities committed by Allied forces at Dresden, Hamburg, Tokyo, Nagasaki, and Hiroshima. We hail the fall of Saddam Hussein without seeing the misery in Fallujah and Baghdad.

Utopian aspirations can tempt us to make moral compromises in order to actualize our ideals. This is the fundamental problem with utilitarianism. It aims to maximize the greatest happiness for the greatest number, while ignoring the suffering of those individuals who are ground under by the social machine. This is what happens when wars of democratization are fought in order to actualize the hope of the democratic peace. And it seems that the more ardently we hope for the actualization of the democratic peace, the more likely we are to make moral compromises. One way of explaining this is that what Yack calls "the longing for total revolution" can lead us to suspend ethics in order to complete the end of history (Yack, 1986).

Idealism has a place. We need to hope for a better world in which more people enjoy what the American Constitution calls "the blessings of liberty." But utilitarian idealism must be circumscribed by a more stringent sort of morality. There are limits to the means that can be employed, even in pursuit of a noble end.

The primary location of such moral limits is in the private voice of individual conscience. States and statesmen operate according to the utilitarian logic of public good. Indeed, we elect them to make decisions based upon the public good. But the cold calculus of public utilitarianism must be criticized, evaluated, and judged from the moral standpoint of private conscience.

Private individuals routinely scream out in protest against the machinery of war. As bombs explode and tear villages apart, mothers and fathers cry out against injustice. As soldiers are conscripted or forced to fight in unjust wars, they object and disobey. And children express their private judgment, folding paper cranes as they die from the ravages of war.

HOPING AGAINST THE DARKNESS

This book has examined a variety of ways that the conflict between public and private is fleshed out in war. Throughout, I have emphasized conflict and tragedy. There is no easy or obvious way to reconcile and resolve the problems we have discussed. This may sound like a dark conclusion. And it is. At one point in history it may have been possible to construct a theodicy in which God provided reconciliation and justification of war. But it has become harder to accept theodicy in the aftermath of the Holocaust, Hiroshima, and the insanity of mutually assured destruction. The leap of faith has become much more difficult for those who would construct a theodicy that would account for genocide and nuclear Armageddon.

The just war theory evolved as a way of finding a space for war within the fundamental pacifism of Christianity. On the one hand, it seems that public duty, discipline, and obedience in the name of the greater good are required. But on the other, there appears to be a higher duty of love and forgiveness. These opposing values are reconciled in the mystery of God, whose forgiveness and justice transcend human understanding.

But by appealing to the mystery of divine love and heavenly justice, we take human judgment out of the equation. From the human standpoint, the problem is knowing how to reconcile the opposing values of public utilitarian concern and private deontological constraint. God may know the proper balance; He may see the big picture in which war and peace are blended together. But we cannot know the divine standpoint.

The best hope for progress is to take seriously the darkness that surrounds us and admit our limitations. Human reason does provide some light. But it is essential to recognize that the light is limited. During the Enlightenment, philosophers and politicians believed that reason would grow in power, gradually illuminating the whole of the world. Progress was indeed made. We have established constitutional systems that protect civil rights. We have abolished slavery and expanded rights to women. We have become more tolerant and more inclusive. We have developed science and technologies that make life easier. But despite the fact that human reason is a genuine engine for progress, it cannot provide a final solution to the human predicament. Indeed, the horrors of the twentieth century can be traced to the dream of final solutions and the demand for absolute and unconditional victory over "the other."

Religious people will claim that this is why we need to return to faith and to the illumination provided by the gods. But the philosophical tradition is more circumspect. The skeptical point of the philosophical tradition is that there is no guarantee of progress, no certainty with regard to justice. Instead, there are conflicting values, which cannot easily be reconciled. The hope is that by recognizing the ubiquity of conflict, we might continue to take care for those values that we cherish most. The hope is that by avoiding easy resolutions and final solutions, we might be more attentive to what is gained and what is lost when we defend the good.

Let me return in conclusion to Sadako Sasaki and her origami cranes. The seemingly futile effort of folding 1,000 paper cranes is at once a tragic and hopeful act. There is no magical act that can overcome the horrors of war and create peace. Sadako died of a war that was fought against the evils of Japanese Imperialism.

But her death remains a reminder of the grinding senselessness of war. Even justifiable wars produce many innocent victims. It may, then, seem easy to give up hope. But without hope, the darkness will surely win. There is a moral imperative to hope for a better world. And hope appears to be expressed best in the private acts of individuals who raise their voices in protest against the paternalist ideal of the public good.

Imagine a 12-year-old girl folding paper cranes at the end of her life. Imagine a conscientious objector testifying in court about the injustice of war. Imagine a voter in the privacy of the voting booth. Imagine a writer at work on a book. Each fold of the paper and each completed crane is a small private act that is oriented toward creating a better world. Rather than giving up in the face of darkness, we must each continue to fold, refold, and create private works of peace and protest. Wars will proceed according to the utilitarian demands of public life. But private individuals retain the power and the responsibility to assert themselves against the grinding logic of war.

BIBLIOGRAPHY

Addams, J. (1911), *Newer Ideals of Peace*. New York: McMillan.

Addams, J. (1922), "President Wilson's policies and the Women's Peace Party," in Jane Addams, *Peace and Bread in Time of War*. New York: Macmillan, 49–72.

Addams, J. (2005a), "Democracy or militarism," in *Writings on Peace: Jane Addams' Essays and Speeches*. London: Continuum, 1–4.

Addams, J. (2005b), "The revolt against war," in Jane Addams, *Writings on Peace: Jane Addam's Essays and Speeches*. London: Continuum, 83–96.

Adorno, T. (1994), *Negative Dialectics*. New York: Continuum.

Alexander, L. (2000), "Deontology at the threshold" *San Diego Law Review* 37:4, 893–912.

Allhoff, F. (2003), "Terrorism and torture" *International Journal of Applied Philosophy* 17:1, 105–118.

Anderson, B. (1983), *Imagined Communities*. London: Verso.

Anscombe, G.E.M. (1981a), "Mr. Truman's degree," in Anscombe *Ethics, Religion, and Politics*. Minneapolis, MN: University of Minnesota Press, 62–71.

Anscombe, G.E.M. (1981b), "War and murder," in Anscombe, *Ethics, Religion, and Politics*. Minneapolis, MN: University of Minnesota Press, 51–71.

Applbaum, A.I. (1992), "Democratic legitimacy and official discretion" *Philosophy and Public Affairs* 21:3, 240–273.

Arendt, H. (1992), *Eichmann in Jerusalem: A Report on the Banality of Evil*. New York: Penguin Classics.

Augustine (408), "Letter to Vincentius." New Advent Church Fathers: www.newadvent.org.

Bacevich, A. (2005), *The New American Militarism: How Americans are Seduced by War*. Oxford: Oxford University Press.

Baracchi, C. (2002), *Of Myth, Life, and War in Plato's Republic*. Bloomington, IN: Indiana University Press.

Becker, L.C. and C.B. Becker (eds.) (2001), *Encyclopedia of Ethics*. New York: Routledge.

Bentham, J. (1843a), "A plan for an universal and perpetual peace," in *Principles of International Law*, from *The Works of Jeremy Bentham*, vol. 2. Edinburgh: William Tait, 546–560.

Bentham, J. (1843b), "Of war: considered in respect of its causes and consequences," in *Principles of International Law*, from *The Works of Jeremy Bentham*, vol. 2. Edinburgh: William Tait, 544–560.

Bentham, J. (1948), *Principles of Morals and Legislation*. New York: Macmillan.

Berlin, I. (1969), "Two concepts of liberty," in Berlin, *Four Essays on Liberty*. Oxford: Oxford University Press.

Bernasconi, R. (2001), *Race*. New York: Blackwell Publishing.

Bertram, C. (1997), "Political justification, theoretical complexity, and democratic control" *Ethics* 107, 563–583.

Bhagavad Gita, (2004), in *Longman Anthology of World Literature, Volume A: The Ancient World*. New York: Pearson/Longman.

Blackburn, S. (2007), *Plato's Republic: A Biography*. New York: Atlantic Monthly Press.

Bourne, R. (1919), "Twilight of the idols," in Bourne, *Untimely Papers*. New York: B.W. Huebsch.

Bourne, R. (1999), *War and the Intellectuals*. Indianapolis, IN: Hackett Publishing, 1999.

Brock, P. (1998), *Varieties of Pacifism: A Survey from Antiquity to the Outset of the Twentieth Century*. Syracuse, NY: Syracuse University Press.

Bufacchi, V. (2005), "Two concepts of violence" *Political Studies Review* 3, 192–204.

Bush, G.W. (2006), *National Security Strategy of the United States (2006)*. White House Archives: www.georgewbush-whitehouse.archives.gov/nsc/nss/2006/nss2006.pdf.

Cady, D. (1990), *From Warism to Pacifism*. Philadelphia, PA: Temple University Press.

Cassirer, E. (1946), *The Myth of the State*. New Haven, CT: Yale University Press.

Catani, C., Schauer, E., Elbert, T., Missmahl, I., Bette, J.P., and Neuner, F. (2009), "War trauma, child labor, and family violence: life adversities and PTSD in a sample of school children in Kabul" *Journal of Traumatic Stress* 22:3 (June), 163–171.

Cheney, D. (2009), "Speech at the American Enterprise Institute," May 21, 2009.

Chomsky, N. (2007), *Failed States*. New York: Macmillan.

Clausewitz, C. von (1982), *On War*. New York: Penguin Books.

Clendenning, J. (1999), *The Life and Thought of Josiah Royce*. Nashville, TN: Vanderbilt University Press.

Cook, M.L. (2004), *The Moral Warrior*. Albany, NY: State University of New York Press.

Cook, M.L. (2008), "The revolt of the generals: a case study in professional ethics" from International Society for Military Ethics: www.usafa.edu/isme/ISME08/Cook08.html.

Craig, L.H. (1994), *The War Lover: A Study of Plato's Republic*. Toronto: University of Toronto Press.

Dallek, R. (2008), *Harry S. Truman*. New York: Macmillan.

Danner, M. (2004), *Torture and Truth*. New York: New York Review Books.

Danner, M. (2009), "U.S. torture: voices from the black sites" *New York Review of Books* (9 April). www.nybooks.com/articles/22530.

Demenchonok, E. (2007), "From a state of war to perpetual peace," in Steven V. Hicks and Daniel E. Shannon (eds), *The Challenges of Globalization: Rethinking Nature, Culture, and Freedom*. Malden, MA: Blackwell Publishing, 25–48.

Dershowitz, A. (2002), *Shouting Fire: Civil Liberties in a Turbulent Age*. New York: Little Brown.

Dewey J. (1983), "Force, violence, and law" in Jo Ann Boydston (ed.), *John Dewey: Middle Works*, vol. 10. Carbondale, IL: Southern Illinois University Press, 211–215.

Dewey, J. (1988), "The lesson from the war—in philosophy," in Jo Ann Boydston (ed.), *John Dewey: Later Works*. Carbondale, IL: Southern Illinois University Press, 315–336.

Dewey, J. (1993a), "Democratic ends require democratic methods for their realization," in Debra Morris and Ian Shapiro (eds), *John Dewey: The Political Writings*. Indianapolis, IN: Hackett, 367–368.

Dewey, J. (2008), "The one-world of Hitler's national socialism," in Jo Ann Boydston (ed.), *John Dewey: Middle Works*, vol. 8. Carbondale, IL: Southern Illinois University Press, 421–448.

Diggins, J.P. (1994), *The Promise of Pragmatism*. Chicago, IL: University of Chicago Press.

Dombrowki, D.A. (1991), *Christian Pacifism*. Philadelphia, PA: Temple University Press.

Dostal, R.J. (2001), "Judging human action: Arendt's appropriation of Kant," in Ronald Beiner and Jennifer Nedelsky (eds.), *Judgment, Imagination, and Politics*. Lanham, MD: Rowman and Littlefield, 139–164.

Doyle, M. (1997), *Ways of War and Peace*. New York: W.W. Norton.

Emerson, R.W. (1911a), "Abraham Lincoln," in *The Works of Ralph Waldo Emerson, vol. 11: Miscellanies*. New York: Houghton Mifflin, 327–338.

Emerson, R.W. (1911b), "John Brown: Boston Speech" (1859) in *The Works of Ralph Waldo Emerson, vol. 11: Miscellanies*. New York: Houghton Mifflin, 267–273.

Emerson, R.W. (1911c), "War," in *The Works of Ralph Waldo Emerson, vol. 11: Miscellanies*. New York: Houghton Mifflin, 149–178.

Emerson, R.W. (1929), "Perpetual forces," in *Lectures and Biographical Sketches* in *The Complete Writings of Ralph Waldo Emerson*, vol. 2. New York: Wm. H. Wise and Co., 967–973.

Emerson, R.W. (2000), "Thoreau," in Brooks Atkinson (ed.), *The Essential Writings of Ralph Waldo Emerson*. New York: Modern Library Classics, 809–828.

Estlund, D. (2007), "On following orders in an unjust war" *The Journal of Political Philosophy* 15:2, 213–234.

Ferrel, R.H. (2008), *Truman and the Bomb*. From Harry Truman On-Line Library: www.trumanlibrary.org/whistlestop/study_collections/bomb/ferrell_book/ferrell_book_chap19.htm.

Fiala, A. (2002a), "The dawning of desire: Hegel's logical history of philosophy and politics," in David Duquette (ed.), *Hegel's History of Philosophy: New Interpretations*. Albany, NY: State University of New York Press, 51–64.

Fiala A. (2002b) *The Philosopher's Voice: Philosophy, Politics, and Language in the Nineteenth Century*. Albany, NY: State University of New York Press.

Fiala, A. (2004), *Practical Pacifism*. New York: Algora Press.

Fiala, A. (2007), *What Would Jesus Really Do?* Lanham, MD: Rowman and Littlefield.

Fiala, A. (2008), *The Just War Myth: The Moral Illusions of War*. Lanham, MD: Rowman and Littlefield.

Flynn, G.Q. (1989), "Selective service and the conscientious objection," in Michael F. Noone, Jr. (ed.), *Selective Conscientious Objector*. Boulder, CO: Westview Press, 35–55.

Frank, J. (2007), "Wages of war" *Political Theory* 35:4 (August), 443–467.

Franklin, B. (1836), "Remarks on Judge Foster's argument in favor of the right of impressing seamen," in Jared Sparks (ed.), *The Works of Benjamin Franklin*. Boston, MA: Hilliar, Gray, and Co., 331–339.

Freedman, B. (1978), "A meta-ethics for professional morality" *Ethics* 89, 1–19.

Fruchtman, J. (2005), *Atlantic Cousins: Benjamin Franklin and His Visionary Friends*. New York: Thunder's Mouth Press.

Fukuyama, F. (1992), *The End of History and the Last Man*. New York: The Free Press.

Fukuyama, F. (2002), "Has history started again?" *Policy* (Winter, 2002), 3–7.

Furtak, R.A. (2003), "Thoreau's emotional stoicism" *Journal of Speculative Philosophy* 17:2, 122–132.

Garcia, J.L.A. (2003), "Some mortal questions: on Justice Scalia and the death penalty" *Logos* 6:2, 125–133.

Gewirth, A. (1986), "Professional ethics: the separatist thesis" *Ethics* 96, 282–300.

Glover, J. (2000), *Humanity: A Moral History of the 20th Century*. New Haven, CT: Yale University Press.

Gorkom, J. van. (2008), "Kant on racial identity" *Philosophy in the Contemporary World* 15:1 (Spring), 1–10.

Gutmann, A. and Thompson, D. (2004), *Why Deliberative Democracy?* Princeton, NJ: Princeton University Press.

Habermas, J. (1991), *The Structural Transformation of the Public Sphere*. Cambridge, MA: MIT Press.

Hadot, P. (2001), *The Inner Citadel: The Meditations of Marcus Aurelius*. Cambridge, MA: Harvard University Press.

Hampshire, S. (2000), *Justice is Conflict*. Princeton, NJ: Princeton University Press.

Hansson, M.G. (2007), *The Private Sphere*. New York: Springer.

Hauerwas, S. (1983), *The Peaceable Kingdom*. Notre Dame, IN: Notre Dame University Press.

Hauerwas, S. (1984), *Should War be Eliminated?* Milwaukee, WI: Marquette University Press.

Hedges, C. (2003), *War is a Force that Gives us Meaning*. New York: Anchor Books.

Hegel, G.W.F. (1956), *Philosophy of History*. New York: Dover.

Hegel, G.W.F. (1961), "The spirit of Christianity and its fate," in T.M. Knox (trans.), *Hegel, On Christianity: Early Theological Writings*. New York: Harper Torchbooks, 182–204.

Hegel, G.W.F. (1977), *Phenomenology of Spirit*. Oxford: Oxford University Press.

Hegel, G.W.F. (1991), *Philosophy of Right*. Cambridge: Cambridge University Press.

Hegel, G.W.F. (1995), *Lectures on Natural Right and Political Science*. Berkeley, CA: University of California Press.

Hegland, C. (2006), "Empty evidence" *National Journal* (Cover Story) February 3, 200638: 5, 28–31.

Hippel, K. von. (2000), *Democracy by Force: U.S. Military Intervention in the Post Cold War World*. Cambridge: Cambridge University Press.

Holborn, H. (1943), "The science of history," in Joseph Strayer (ed.), *The Interpretation of History*. Princeton, NJ: Princeton University Press, 59–84.

Holmes, R. (1989), *On War and Morality*. Princeton, NJ: Princeton University Press.

Homer, (1990), *Iliad*. New York: Penguin Books.

Huntington, Samuel P. (1957), *The Soldier and the State: The Theory and Politics of Civil-Military Relations*. Cambridge, MA: Harvard University Press.

Huntington, Samuel P. (1996), *The Clash of Civilizations*. New York: Simon and Schuster.

Hyppolite, J. (1996), *Introduction to Hegel's Philosophy of History*. Gainesville, FL: University of Florida Press.

Ignatieff, M. (1995), "The myth of citizenship," in Ronald Beiner (ed.), *Theorizing Citizenship*. Albany, NY: State University of New York Press, 53–78.

Ignatieff, M. (2004), *The Lesser Evil*. Princeton, NJ: Princeton University Press.

Jackson, T.F. (2007), *From Civil Rights to Human Rights: Martin Luther King, Jr., and the Struggle for Economic Justice*. Philadelphia, PA: University of Pennsylvania Press.

James, W. (1987), *Writings: 1902–1910*. Bruce Kuklick (ed.), New York: Library of America, 1281–1293.

Jeffreys, D. (2006), "Eliminating all empathy: personalism and the war on terror" *Logos* 9:3 (Summer), 16–44.

Johnson, J.T. (1981), *Just War Tradition and the Restraint of War*. Princeton, NJ: Princeton University Press.

Journals of the Continental Congress. The Library of Congress American Memory Project: www.memory.loc.gov/ammem/index.html.

Kant, I. (1887), *The Philosophy of Law.* Edinburgh: T&T Clark.

Kant, I. (1965a), *Critique of Pure Reason.* New York: St. Martin's Press.

Kant, I. (1965b), *Metaphysical Elements of Justice (Rechtslehre* from the *Metaphysics of Morals).* New York: Macmillan.

Kant, I. (1970), *Critique of Judgment.* New York: Hafner Library of Classics.

Kant, I. (1991a), *Conjectures on the Beginning of Human History* in H.S. Reiss (ed.), *Kant, Political Writings.* Cambridge: Cambridge University Press, 221–234.

Kant, I. (1991b), *Idea for a Universal History* in H.S. Reiss (ed.), *Kant, Political Writings.* Cambridge: Cambridge University Press, 41–53.

Kant, I. (1991c), *Metaphysics of Morals* in H.S. Reiss (ed.), *Kant, Political Writings.* Cambridge: Cambridge University Press, 131–175.

Kant, I. (1991d), *Perpetual Peace* in H.S. Reiss (ed.), *Kant, Political Writings.* Cambridge: Cambridge University Press, 93–130.

Kant, I. (1991e), "What is enlightenment?" in H.S. Reiss (ed.), *Kant, Political Writings.* Cambridge: Cambridge University Press, 54–60.

Kant, I. (1998a), *Groundwork of the Metaphysics of Morals.* Cambridge: Cambridge University Press.

Kant, I. (1998b), *Religion within the Boundaries of Mere Reason.* Cambridge: Cambridge University Press.

Kant, I. (2004), *Observations on the Beautiful and the Sublime.* Berkeley, CA: University of California Press.

Kaplan, R.D. (2002), *Warrior Politics.* New York: Vintage Books.

Ketcham, R.L. (1990), *James Madison.* Charlottesville, VA: University of Virginia Press.

King, M.L. Jr. (1963), "Letter from Birmingham Jail." From King Archive: www.kingpapers.org.

Kinzer, S. (2006), *Overthrow: America's Century of Regime Change from Hawaii to Iraq.* New York: Macmillan.

Kohn, R.H. (1997), "How democracies control the military" *Journal of Democracy* 8:4, 141.

Kojève, A. (1969), *Introduction to the Study of Hegel.* New York: Basic Books.

Lachs, J. (2005), "Stoic pragmatism" *Journal of Speculative Philosophy* 19:2, 95–106.

Lackey, D. (2003), "Why Hiroshima was immoral: a response to Landesman" *Philosophical Forum* 34:1 (Spring), 39–42.

Landesman, C. (2003), "Rawls on Hiroshima: an inquiry into the morality of the use of atomic weapons in August 1945" *Philosophical Forum* 34:1 (Spring), 21–38.

Lesnor, C. (2005), "The 'good war'" *Philosophical Forum* 36:1 (Spring), 77–85.

Machiavelli, N. (1988), *The Prince.* Cambridge: Cambridge University Press.

Mackie, J.L. (1977), *Ethics.* New York: Penguin Books.

Madison, James (1795/1865), "Political observations," in James Madison, *Letters and Other Writings* vol. 4. Philadelphia, PA: J.B. Lippincott, 485–505.

Marcuse, H. (1983), *Reason and Revolution*. Atlantic Highland, NJ: Humanities Press.

May, L. (2007), *War Crimes and Just Wars*. Cambridge: Cambridge University Press.

Menand, L (2002), *The Metaphysical Club*. New York: Macmillan.

Mill, J.S. (1984), "A Few Words on Nonintervention," in John M. Robinson (ed.), *The Collected Works of John Stuart Mill*, vol. XXI. Toronto: University of Toronto Press, 109–124.

Mill, J.S. (1998a), *On Liberty* in John Gray (ed.), *On Liberty and Other Essays*. Oxford: Oxford University Press, 5–130.

Mill, J.S. (1998b), *Considerations on Representative Government* in John Gray (ed.), *On Liberty and Other Essays*. Oxford: Oxford University Press, 205–470.

Mill, J.S. (1998c), *Utilitarianism* in John Stuart Mill (ed.), *On Liberty and Other Essays*. Oxford: Oxford University Press, 205–470.

Miller R.B. (1991), *Interpretations of Conflict*. Chicago, IL: University of Chicago Press.

Murphy, A. (2002), *To Hell and Back*. New York: Macmillan Reprint.

Nietzsche, F. (1968), *The Will to Power*. New York: Vintage Books.

Nixon, R. (1970), "Message to Congress on draft reform" (April 23, 1970). The American Presidency Project: www.presidency.ucsb.edu/ws/index.php?pid=2483.

Noone, M.F., Jr. (1989), *Selective Conscientious Objection: Accommodating Conscience and Security*. Boulder, CO: Westview Press.

Nussbaum, M. (2005), "Women's bodies: violence, security, and capabilities" *Journal of Human Development* 6:2, 167–183.

Nussbaum, M. (2008), *Liberty of Conscience*. New York: Perseus Books.

Orend, B. (2000), *War and International Justice: A Kantian Perspective*. Waterloo: Wilfred Laurier University Press.

Pinkard, T. (2001), *Hegel: A Biography*. Cambridge: Cambridge University Press.

Plato, (1989), *Collected Dialogues*. Princeton, NJ: Princeton University Press.

Popper, K. (1971), *The Open Society and its Enemies*. Princeton, NJ: Princeton University Press.

Porter, B.D. (1994), *War and the Rise of the State*. New York: The Free Press.

Ramsey, P. (1968), *The Just War*. New York: Scribners.

Ramsey, P. (1985), *War and the Christian Conscience*. Durham, NC: Duke University Press.

Rawls, J. (1971), *A Theory of Justice*. Cambridge, MA: Harvard University Press.

Rawls, J. (1999a), "Fifty years after Hiroshima," in Rawls, *Collected Papers*. Cambridge, MA: Harvard University Press, 565–572.

Rawls, J. (1999b), *The Law of Peoples*. Cambridge, MA: Harvard University Press.

Recco, G. (2007), *Athens Victorious: Democracy in Plato's Republic*. New York: Lexington Books.

Reiman, J. (1985), "Justice, civilization, and the death penalty" *Philosophy and Public Affairs* 14, 119–134.

Roosevelt, F.D. "First Inaugural Address." *Bartleby's Inaugural Addresses of the Presidents of the United State*. www.bartleby.com/124/pres49.html.

Roosevelt, T. (1897), "Naval War College Address." www.theodore-roosevelt.com/tr1898.html.

Roosevelt, T. (1905a), "Grant," in *The Strenuous Life: Essays and Addresses*. New York: Century, 207–228.

Roosevelt, T. (1905b), "The Strenuous Life," in *The Strenuous Life: Essays and Addresses*. New York: Century, 1–24.

Roosevelt, T. (1915), *America and the The World War*. New York: Charles Scribners.

Ross, W.D. (1930), *The Right and the Good*. Oxford: Clarendon Press.

Rousseau, J.J. (1967), *The Social Contract* in Jean-Jacques Rousseau, *The Social Contract and Discourse on the Origin of Inequality*. New York: Washington Square Press, 3–150.

Rousseau, J.J. (2006), "Critique of the Abbé de Saint-Pierre's Project for Perpetual Peace and Summary of the Abbé de Saint-Pierre's Project for Perpetual Peace" in Gregory M. Reichberg, Henrik Syse, Endre Begby (eds.), *The Ethics of War*. New York: Wiley-Blackwell, 490–503.

Royce, J. (1916), *War and Insurance*. New York: Macmillan.

Royce, J. (1995), *The Philosophy of Loyalty*. Nashville, TN: Vanderbilt University Press.

Rummel, R.J. (1997), *Power Kills: Democracy as a Method of Nonviolence*. New Brunswick, NJ: Transaction Publishers.

Sandburg, C. (1936), "Little girl saw her first troop parade," in *The People, Yes*. New York: Harcourt, Brace and Co.

Santayana, G. (1937), *The Works of George Santayana*. New York: Scribners.

Santayana, G. (1986), *Persons and Places*. Cambridge, MA: MIT Press.

Scarry, E. (1985), *The Body in Pain*. Oxford: Oxford University Press.

Seneca, (1958), *The Stoic Philosophy of Seneca*. New York: Norton.

Sharlet, J. (2009), "Jesus killed Mohammed: the crusade for a Christian military" *Harpers* (May), 31–43.

Sharp, G. (1773), *Remarks on Crown Law*. London: B. White & R. Horsfield.

Shue, H. (1978), "Torture" *Philosophy and Public Affairs* 7:2 (Winter), 124–143.

Shue, H. (2004), "Liberalism: the impossibility of justifying weapons of mass destruction," in Sohail H. Hashmi and Steven Lee (eds), *Ethics and Weapons of Mass Destruction*. Cambridge: Cambridge University Press, 139–162.

Singer, P.W. (2004), "The private military industry and Iraq." Geneva Center for the Democratic Control of the Armed Forces: www.dcaf. ch/_docs/pp04_private-military.pdf.

Spiner, J. (1994), *The Boundaries of Citizenship*. Baltimore, MD: Johns Hopkins University Press.

Taurek, J. (1977), "Should the numbers count?" *Philosophy and Public Affairs* 6:4, 293–316.

Teichman, J. (1986), *Pacifism and the Just War*. Oxford: Basil Blackwell.

Teson, F. (1998), *A Philosophy of International Law*. Boulder, CO: Westview Press.

Thoreau, H.D. (1906), *The Writings of Henry David Thoreau*. New York: Houghton Mifflin Co.

Thoreau, H.D. (2000a), "A Plea for Captain John Brown," in Brooks Atkinson (ed.), *Walden and Other Writings*. New York: Modern Library, 715–744.

Thoreau, H.D. (2000b), "Civil Disobedience," in Brooks Atkinson (ed.), *Walden and Other Writings*. New York: Modern Library, 665–694.

Tocqueville, A. (2002), *Democracy in America*. Chicago, IL: University of Chicago Press.

Turner, F.J. (1896),"The Problem of the West" *The Atlantic* (September). From Atlantic.com archive: www.theatlantic.com/issues/95sep/ets/turn. htm

Twain, M. (1992a), "Battle hymn of the republic (brought down to date)," in Twain, *Collected Tales, Sketches, Speeches and Essays: 1891–1910*, vol. 2. New York: Library of America, 474–475.

Twain, M. (1992b), "The war prayer" in Twain, *Collected Tales, Sketches, Speeches and Essays: 1891–1910*, vol. 2. New York: Library of America, 652–655.

Twain, M. (1992c), "To the person sitting in darkness," in Twain, *Collected Tales, Sketches, Speeches and Essays: 1891–1910*, vol. 2. New York: Library of America, 457–473.

Tyler, C. (2004), "Hegel, war and the tragedy of imperialism," in *History of European Ideas* 30: 4, 403–431.

UN Commission on Human Rights (1997), "The question of conscientious objection to military service." www.hri.ca/fortherecord1997/documen- tation/commission/e-cn4-1997-99.htm.

UNICEF (2007), "Child alert on Afghanistan." www.unicef.org/childalert/ afghanistan/Child_Alert_Afghanistan_Oct2007.pdf

Valls, A. (2006), "Can terrorism be justified?" in Larry May, Eric Rovie, and Steve Viner (eds.), *The Morality of War*. New York: Pearson/Prentice Hall, 315–325.

Wagner, R.H. (2007), *War and the State*. Ann Arbor, MI: University of Michigan Press.

Waltz, K. (1962), "Kant, liberalism, and war" *American Political Science Review* 56:2, 331–340.

Walzer, M. (1973), "Political action: the problem of dirty hands" *Philosophy and Public Affairs* 2:2 (Winter), 160–180.

Walzer, M. (1977), *Just and Unjust Wars*. New York: Basic Books.

Walzer, M. (1995), "The civil society argument," in Ronald Beiner (ed.), *Theorizing Citizenship*. Albany, NY: State University of New York Press, 153–174.

Walzer, M. (2004), *Arguing About War*. New Haven, CT: Yale University Press.

Walzer, M. (2006), "Terrorism: a critique of excuses," in Larry May, Eric Rovie, and Steve Viner (eds.), *The Morality of War*. New York: Pearson/ Prentice Hall.

Watner, C. (1980), "In favorem libertatis: the life and times of Granville Sharp" *The Journal of Libertarian Studies* 4:2 (Spring), 215–252.

Watt, S.L. (2003), *Rough Rider in the White House*. Chicago, IL: University of Chicago Press.

Weart, S.R. (1998), *Never at War: Why Democracies Will Not Fight One Another*. New Haven, CT: Yale University Press.

Weber, M. (1950), *General Economic History*. New York: The Free Press.

Weigel, G. (1987), *Tranquillitas Ordinis: The Present Failure and Future Promise of American Catholic Thought on War and Peace*. Oxford: Oxford University Press.

Weil, S. (2003), *The Iliad or The Poem of Force*. New York: Peter Lang Publishing.

West, C. (1989), *The American Evasion of Philosophy*. Madison, WI: University of Wisconsin Press.

Wilson, W. (1917), "President Woodrow Wilson's proclamation establishing conscription" (May 28, 1917). www.firstworldwar.com/ www.firstworldwar.com/source/usconscription_wilson.htm.

Yack, B. (1986), *The Longing for Total Revolution*. Berkeley, CA: University of California Press.

Yoder, J.H. (2003), *The Original Revolution*. Scottdale, PA: Herald Press.

Zahn, G. (1989), "A pacifist's view of conscientious objection," in Michael F. Noone, Jr. (ed.), *Selective Conscientious Objection*. Boulder, CO: Westview, 57–62.

Zinn, H. (2005), *A People's History of the United States*. New York: HarperPerennial Modern Classics.

Zupan, D.S. (2004), *War, Morality and Autonomy*. Burlington, VT: Ashgate.

INDEX